Introduction to C++

A Short Guide to Programming in C++

Microsoft Corporation

Document No. DB69754-0296
Printed in the United States of America

Contents

Part 1 Basic C++

Part 2   Classes   37

Chapter 6   More Features of Classes 89

Chapter 7   Inheritance and Polymorphism   113

Part 3   Object-Oriented Design   167

Part 4 Appendixes 191

Figures and Tables

Figures

Tables

Introduction

Introduction to C++

This book provides an introduction to the C++ language and object-oriented programming. The main body of this book assumes you are familiar with C, and therefore doesn't cover the parts of the C++ language that are also found in C. In some places, this book compares C++ with C in order to demonstrate how the same problem might be solved in each language.

If you've previously learned C but haven't programmed in it recently, you can consult the appendixes for a quick refresher. Appendix A provides a quick summary of the C language, while Appendix B describes some of the common mistakes people make when first programming in C.

This book is not an exhaustive description of the C++ language. It teaches the major features of C++ and gives examples of how they can be used. For more detailed information on C++, see the *C++ Language Reference* online.

About This Book

The following list summarizes the book's contents:

- Part 1, "Basic C++," describes some of the simple enhancements that C++ has made to C. These features are not object-oriented, but they provide conveniences that C programmers can readily appreciate.

- Part 2, "Classes," covers the most important elements of C++: classes, inheritance, and polymorphism. These features are what make C++ an object-oriented language.

- Part 3, "Object-Oriented Design," covers the conceptual aspects of object-oriented programming. This section describes the steps in designing an object-oriented program.
- Part 4, "Appendixes," contains summary information on C programming.

You should read the chapters in order, because each one assumes that you know the material covered in previous chapters.

Document Conventions

This book has the following typographic conventions:

Example	Description
STDIO.H	Uppercase letters indicate filenames, segment names, registers, and terms used at the operating-system command level.
expression	Words in italics indicate placeholders for information you must supply, such as a filename. Italic type is also occasionally used for emphasis in the text.
char, **_setcolor**, **__far**	Bold type indicates keywords, operators, language-specific characters, and library routines. Within discussions of syntax, bold type indicates the text must be entered exactly as shown.
	Many functions and constants begin with either a single or double underscore. These are part of the name and are mandatory. For example, to have the **__cplusplus** manifest constant be recognized by the compiler, you must enter the leading double underscore.
[*option*]	Items inside square brackets are optional.
**#pragma pack {1	2}**	Braces and a vertical bar indicate a choice among two or more items. You must choose one of these items unless square brackets surround the braces: [{	}].
`#include <io.h>`	This font is used for examples, user input, program output, and error messages in text.
CL [*option...*] *file...*	Three dots (an ellipsis) following an item indicate that more items having the same form can appear.

Example	Description
| ```
while()
{
    .
    .
    .
}
``` | A column or row of three dots tells you that part of an example program has been intentionally omitted. |
CTRL+ENTER	Small capital letters are used to indicate the names of keys on the keyboard. When you see a plus sign (+) between two key names, you should hold down the first key while pressing the second.
	The carriage-return key, sometimes marked as a bent arrow on the keyboard, is called ENTER.
"argument"	Quotation marks enclose a new term the first time it is defined in text.
`"C string"`	Some C constructs, such as strings, require quotation marks.
Color/Graphics Adapter (CGA)	The first time an acronym is used, it is usually spelled out.
```

Basic C++

A First Look at C++

The C++ language is derived from C. With few exceptions, it is a superset of C, meaning that everything available in C is also available in C++. C++ adds some simple enhancements to C's own features and some major new features that don't exist in C.

This chapter covers some of the differences in conventions between C and C++. It begins with a new way of handling input and output, which you'll need to know for later programs that print results on the screen. This chapter also covers C++ comments and function prototypes.

Using Streams for Input and Output

Here is HELLO.CPP, a very simple C++ program:

```
#include <iostream.h>
void main()
{
    cout << "Hello, world\n";
}
```

This program is the C++ version of the C program HELLO.C. However, instead of including STDIO.H, the program includes IOSTREAM.H, and instead of a **printf** call, it uses an unfamiliar syntax with an undefined variable named **cout**, the bitwise left shift operator (<<), and a string.

Note   Visual C++ Standard Edition Version 4.0 uses "project workspaces" to manage the files that get compiled into an executable program. These are similar to the makefiles you may have used with a command-line compiler, except that you create and edit them from within the Visual C++ environment.

Before you can compile and run a program like HELLO.CPP from within Visual C++ 4.0's environment, the file must be part of a project workspace. You can create a project workspace consisting of a single file by performing the following steps:

1. From the File menu, choose New.

2. In the dialog box that appears, select Text File and choose OK.

3. In the editor window that appears, type the code for your program.

4. From the Build menu, choose Build. A dialog box appears, asking if you want to create a default project workspace.

5. Choose Yes. The Save As dialog box appears.

6. In the Save As dialog box, type the name under which the file should be saved.

7. Choose Save. The Visual C++ environment now saves the file as its own project workspace and compiles it.

8. From the Build menu, choose Execute. The program now runs.

In Visual C++ Standard Edition 4.0, each program must have its own project workspace. Most of the examples shown in this book consist of only one file, so the procedure described above will work for those examples. Later in this book, you'll learn how to add files to an existing project workspace, so that multiple files get compiled into a single executable program.

For more information on project workspaces, see the "Working with projects" topic in Books Online. If you're using Visual C++ 1.52, you can compile single-file programs without creating a project.

The Standard Output Stream

In C++, there are facilities for performing input and output known as "streams." The example programs throughout this book use streams to read and display information. The name **cout** represents the standard output stream. For example:

```
cout << "Hello, world\n";
```

The string "Hello, world\n" is sent to the standard output device, which is the screen. The **<<** operator is called the "insertion" operator. It points from what is being sent (the string) to where it is going (the screen).

Suppose you want to print an integer instead of a string. In C, you would use **printf** with a format string that describes the parameters:

```
printf( "%d\n", amount );
```

In C++, you don't need the format string:

```
#include <iostream.h>

void main()
{
    int amount = 123;
    cout << amount << endl;
}
```

The program prints 123. Note that the **cout** statement ends with << endl, which is the equivalent of printing a '\n' character. You can use endl or '\n' interchangeably to print a newline character.

You can send any built-in data types to the output stream without a format string. The **cout** stream is aware of the different data types and interprets them correctly.

The following example shows how to send a string, an integer, and a character constant to the output stream using one statement:

```
#include <iostream.h>

void main()
{
    int amount = 123;
    cout << "The value of amount is " << amount << '.' << endl;
}
```

This program sends three different data types to **cout**: a string literal, the integer amount variable, and a character constant '.' to add a period to the end of the sentence. The program prints this message:

```
The value of amount is 123.
```

Notice how multiple values are displayed using a single statement: The << operator is repeated for each value.

Formatted Output

So far, the examples haven't sent formatted output to **cout**. Suppose you want to display an integer using hexadecimal instead of decimal notation. The **printf** function handles this well. How does **cout** do it?

Note Whenever you wonder how to get C++ to do something that C does, remember that the entire C language is part of C++. In the absence of a better way, you can revert to C.

C++ associates a set of "manipulators" with the output stream. They change the default format for integer arguments. You insert the manipulators into the stream to make the change. The manipulators' names are **dec**, **oct**, and **hex**.

The next example shows how you can display an integer value in its three possible configurations:

```
#include <iostream.h>

main()
{
    int amount = 123;
    cout << dec << amount << ' '
         << oct << amount << ' '
         << hex << amount << endl;
}
```

The example inserts each of the manipulators (**dec**, **oct**, and **hex**) to convert the value in amount into different representations.

This program prints this:

```
123 173 7b
```

Each of the values shown is a different representation of the decimal value 123 from the amount variable.

The Standard Error Stream

To send output to the standard error device, use **cerr** instead of **cout**. You can use this technique to send messages to the screen from programs that have their standard output redirected to another file or device.

The Standard Input Stream

In addition to printing messages, you may want to read data from the keyboard. C++ includes its own version of standard input in the form of **cin**. The next example shows you how to use **cin** to read an integer from the keyboard:

```
#include <iostream.h>

void main()
{
    int amount;
    cout << "Enter an amount...\n";
    cin >> amount;
    cout << "The amount you entered was " << amount << endl;
}
```

This example prompts you to enter an amount. Then **cin** sends the value that you enter to the variable amount. The next statement displays the amount, using **cout** to demonstrate that the **cin** operation worked.

You can use **cin** to read other data types as well. The next example shows how to read a string from the keyboard:

```
#include <iostream.h>

void main()
{
    char name[20];
    cout << "Enter a name...\n";
    cin >> name;
    cout << "The name you entered was " << name << endl;
}
```

Note that the approach shown in this example has a serious flaw in that the character array is only 20 characters long. If you type too many characters, the stack overflows and peculiar things happen. The **cout** stream defines a **get** function which solves this problem; it's explained in the *iostream Reference* online. For now, the examples assume that you will not type more characters than a string can accept.

Note   Recall that **printf** and **scanf** are not part of the C language proper but are functions defined in the run-time library. Similarly, the **cin** and **cout** streams are not part of the C++ language. Instead, they are defined in the stream library, which is why you must include IOSTREAM.H in order to use them. Furthermore, the meaning of the **<<** and **>>** operators depends on the context in which they are used. They can display or read data only when used with **cout** and **cin**.

C++ Comments

C++ supports the C comment format where /* begins a comment and */ ends it. But C++ has another comment format, which is preferred by many programmers. The C++ comment token is the double-slash (//) sequence. Wherever this sequence appears (unless it is inside a string), everything to the end of the current line is a comment.

The next example adds comments to the previous program:

```
// C++ comments
#include <iostream.h>

void main()
{
    char name[20];               // Declare a string
    cout << "Enter a name...\n"; // Request a name
    cin >> name;                 // Read the name
    cout << "The name you entered was " << name << endl;
}
```

Function Prototypes

In standard C, you can declare a function before you define it. The declaration describes the function's name, its return value, and the number and types of its parameters. This feature, called a "function prototype," allows the compiler to compare the function calls to the prototype and to enforce type checking.

C does not require a prototype for each function. If you omit it, at worst you get a warning. C++, on the other hand, requires every function to have a prototype.

The next example uses a function named display to print "Hello, world":

```
// A program without function prototypes
// Note: This will not compile.
#include <iostream.h>

void main()
{
    display( "Hello, world\n" );
}

void display( char *s )
{
    cout << s;
}
```

Because the display function has no prototype, this program does not survive the syntax-checking phase of the C++ compiler.

The next example adds a function prototype to the previous program (now the program compiles without errors):

```
// A program with a function prototype
#include <iostream.h>

void display( char *s );

void main()
{
    display( "Hello, world\n" );
}

void display( char *s )
{
    cout << s;
}
```

In some C programs, the function definitions declare the types of the parameters between the parameter list and the function body. C++ requires that function definitions declare the types of all parameters within the parameter list. For example:

```
void display( char *s )  // New style required in C++
{
    cout << s;
}

void display( s )        // Error: old style doesn't work
char *s
{
    cout << s;
}
```

If you define a function before you call it, you don't need a separate prototype; the function definition acts as the prototype. However, if you don't define the function until after you call it, or if the function is defined in another file, you must provide a prototype.

Keep in mind that the prototype requirement is an exception to the general rule that a C++ compiler can handle a C program. If your C programs do not have function prototypes and new-style function-declaration blocks, then you must add them before compiling the programs in C++.

Note   If you need to generate new-style function prototypes for existing C programs, use the CL.EXE program with the /Zg command-line option. In Visual C++ Standard Edition 4.0, see the "CL Reference" in the online *Visual C++ User's Guide* for more details.

C++ Enhancements to C

This chapter introduces some simple enhancements and improvements that C++ offers the C programmer. New features covered in this chapter include the following:

- Default function arguments
- More flexible placement of variable declarations
- The scope resolution operator
- Inline functions
- The **const** keyword
- Enumerations
- Function overloading

This chapter also describes how to link C and C++ modules together.

Default Function Arguments

A C++ function prototype can list default values for some of the parameters. If you omit the corresponding arguments when you call the function, the compiler automatically uses the default values. If you provide your own arguments, the compiler uses them instead of the defaults. The following prototype illustrates this feature:

```
void myfunc( int i = 5, double d = 1.23 );
```

Here, the numbers 5 and 1.23 are the default values for the parameters. You could call the function in several ways:

```
myfunc( 12, 3.45 );   // Overrides both defaults
myfunc( 3 );          // Same as myfunc( 3, 1.23 )
myfunc();             // Same as myfunc( 5, 1.23 )
```

If you omit the first argument, you must omit all arguments that follow. You can omit the second argument, however, and override the default for the first. This rule applies to any number of arguments. You cannot omit an argument unless you omit all the arguments to its right. For example, the following function call is illegal:

```
myfunc( , 3.5 );    // Error: cannot omit only first argument
```

A syntax like this is error-prone and makes reading and writing function calls more difficult.

The following example uses default arguments in the show function.

```
// DEFARG.CPP: A program with default arguments in a function prototype
#include <iostream.h>

void show( int first = 1, double second = 2.3, long third = 4 );

void main()
{
    show();                 // All three arguments default
    show( 5 );              // Provide 1st argument
    show( 6, 7.8 );         // Provide 1st and 2nd
    show( 9, 10.11, 12L );  // Provide all three arguments
}

void show( int first, double second, long third )
{
    cout <<    "first = " << first;
    cout << ", second = " << second;
    cout <<   ", third = " << third << endl;
}
```

When you run this example, it prints:

```
first = 1, second = 2.3, third = 4
first = 5, second = 2.3, third = 4
first = 6, second = 7.8, third = 4
first = 9, second = 10.11, third = 12
```

Default values provide a lot of flexibility. For example, if you usually call a function using the same argument values, you can put them in the prototype and later call the function without supplying the arguments. The only time you need to specify arguments is when they differ from the default values.

Placement of Variable Declarations

C requires you to declare variables at the beginning of a block. In C++, you can declare a variable anywhere in the code, as long as you declare it before you reference it. Using this feature, you can place the declaration of a variable closer to the code that uses it, making the program more readable.

The following example shows how you can position the declaration of a variable near its first reference:

```
// Declaring a variable near its first reference
#include <iostream.h>

void main()
{
    cout << "Enter a number: ";
    int n;
    cin >> n;
    cout << "The number is: " << n << endl;
}
```

The freedom to declare a variable anywhere in a block makes expressions such as the following one possible:

```
for( int ctr = 0; ctr < MAXCTR; ctr++ )
```

However, you cannot have expressions such as the following:

```
if( int i == 0 )        // Error
    ;
while( int j == 0 )     // Error
    ;
```

Such expressions are meaningless, because there is no need to test the value of a variable the moment it is declared.

The following example declares a variable in a block:

```
// VARDECL.CPP: Variable declaration placement
#include <iostream.h>

void main()
{
    for( int lineno = 0; lineno < 3; lineno++ )
    {
        int temp = 22;
        cout << "This is line number " << lineno
            << " and temp is " << temp << endl;
    }
    if( lineno == 4 )   // lineno still accessible
        cout << "Oops\n";
    // Cannot access temp
}
```

This example produces the following output:

```
This is line number 0 and temp is 22
This is line number 1 and temp is 22
This is line number 2 and temp is 22
```

Note that the two variables lineno and temp have different scopes. The lineno variable is in scope for the current block (in this case, until **main** ends) and for all blocks subordinate to the current one. The lineno variable's scope does not begin until its declaration. C++ statements that appear before a variable's declaration cannot refer to the variable even though they appear in the same block. The temp variable goes out of scope when the **for** loop ends. It is accessible only from within the loop.

You should exercise care when declaring variables in places other than the beginning of a block. If you scatter declarations haphazardly throughout your program, a person reading your program may have difficulty finding where a variable is declared.

The Scope Resolution Operator

In C, a local variable takes precedence over a global variable with the same name. For example, if both a local variable and a global variable are called count, all occurrences of count while the local variable is in scope refer to the local variable. It's as if the global variable becomes invisible.

In C++, you can tell the compiler to use the global variable rather than the local one by prefixing the variable with **::**, the scope resolution operator. For example:

```
// SCOPERES.CPP: Scope resolution operator
#include <iostream.h>

int amount = 123;    // A global variable

void main()
{
   int amount = 456; // A local variable

   cout << ::amount << endl; // Print the global variable
   cout <<   amount << endl; // Print the local variable
}
```

The example has two variables named `amount`. The first is global and contains the value 123. The second is local to the **main** function. The two colons tell the compiler to use the global `amount` instead of the local one. The program prints this on the screen:

```
123
456
```

Note that if you have nested local scopes, the scope resolution operator doesn't provide access to variables in the next outermost scope. It provides access to only the global variables.

The scope resolution operator gives you more freedom in naming your variables by letting you distinguish between variables with the same name. However, you shouldn't overuse this feature; if two variables have different purposes, their names should reflect that difference.

Inline Functions

C++ provides the **inline** keyword as a function qualifier. This keyword causes a new copy of the function to be inserted in each place it is called. If you call an inline function from 20 places in your program, the compiler inserts 20 copies of that function into your .EXE file.

Inserting individual copies of functions eliminates the overhead of calling a function (such as loading parameters onto the stack), so your program runs faster. However, having multiple copies of a function can make your program larger.

You should use the **inline** function qualifier only when the inserted function is very small or is called from few places.

Inline functions are similar to macros declared with the **#define** directive; however, inline functions are recognized by the compiler, while macros are implemented by a simple text substitution. One advantage of this is that the compiler performs type checking on the parameters of an inline function. Another advantage is that an inline function behaves just as an ordinary function does, without any of the side effects that macros have. For example:

```
// INLINE.CPP: A macro vs. an inline function
#include <iostream.h>

#define MAX( A, B ) ((A) > (B) ? (A) : (B))

inline int max( int a, int b )
{
    if ( a > b ) return a;
    return b;
}

void main()
{
    int i, x, y;

    x = 23; y = 45;
    i = MAX( x++, y++ );   // Side-effect:
                           //    larger value incremented twice
    cout << "x = " << x << " y = " << y << endl;

    x = 23; y = 45;
    i = max( x++, y++ );   // Works as expected
    cout << "x = " << x << " y = " << y << endl;
}
```

This example prints the following:

```
x = 24 y = 47
x = 24 y = 46
```

If you want a function like max to accept arguments of any type, the way a macro does, you can use overloaded functions. These are described in the section "Overloaded Functions" later in this chapter.

To be safe, always declare inline functions before you make any calls to them. If an inline function is to be called by code in several source files, put its declaration in a header file. Any modifications to the body of an inline function require recompilation of all the files that call that function.

The **inline** keyword is only a suggestion to the compiler. Functions larger than a few lines are not expanded inline even if they are declared with the **inline** keyword.

Note   The Microsoft Visual C++ compiler supports the **__inline** keyword for C, which has the same meaning as **inline** does in C++.

The const Qualifier

C++, like C, supports the **const** qualifier, which turns variables into constants. In C, the **const** qualifier specifies that a variable is read-only, except during its one-time initialization. Only through initialization can a program specify a **const** variable's value. C++ goes a step further and treats such variables as if they are true constant expressions (such as 123). Wherever you can use a constant expression, you can use a **const** variable. For example:

```
// CONST.CPP: The const qualifier
#include <iostream.h>

void main()
{
    const int SIZE = 5;
    char cs[SIZE];

    cout << "The size of cs is " << sizeof cs << endl;
}
```

This program is illegal in C, because C does not let you use a **const** variable to specify the size of an array. However, even in C++ you cannot initialize a **const** variable with anything other than a constant expression. For example, even though SIZE is declared within a function, you cannot initialize it with a parameter of the function. This means you cannot use **const** to declare an array whose size is determined at run time. To dynamically allocate an array in C++, see Chapter 5, "Classes and Dynamic Memory Allocation."

You can use **const** declarations as a replacement for constants defined with the **#define** directive. C++ lets you place **const** declarations in header files, which is illegal in C. (If you try doing this in C, the linker generates error messages if the header file is included by more than one module in a program.) Constants declared with **const** have an advantage over those defined by **#define** in that they are accessible to a symbolic debugger, making debugging easier.

You can also use **const** in pointer declarations. In such declarations, the placement of **const** is significant. For example:

```
char *const ptr = mybuf;   // const pointer
                           // First change char that pointer points to
*ptr = 'a';                // Okay
                           // Now try to change pointer itself
ptr = yourbuf;             // Error: ptr is const
```

This declares `ptr` as a constant pointer to a string. You can modify the string that `ptr` points to, but you cannot modify `ptr` itself by making it point to another string.

However, the following declaration has a different meaning:

```
const char *ptr = mybuf;   // Pointer to const

                           // First change pointer itself
ptr = yourbuf;             // Okay
                           // Now try to change char that pointer points to
*ptr = 'a';                // Error: *ptr is const
```

This declares `ptr` as a pointer to a constant string. You can modify `ptr` itself so that it points to another string, but you cannot modify the string that `ptr` points to. In effect, this makes `ptr` a "read-only" pointer.

You can use **const** when declaring a function to prevent the function from modifying one of its parameters. Consider the following prototype:

```
struct Node;     // Node is a large structure

void readonly( const struct Node *nodeptr );
```

This prototype declares that the `readonly` function cannot modify the `Node` structure that its parameter points to. Even if an ordinary pointer is declared inside the function, the parameter is still safeguarded, because you cannot assign a read-only pointer to an ordinary pointer. For example:

```
struct Node;     // Node is a large structure

void readonly( const struct Node *nodeptr )
{
    struct Node *writeptr;  // Ordinary pointer (allows read/write)

    writeptr = nodeptr;     // Error: can't assign const to non-const
}
```

If such an assignment were legal, the `Node` structure could be modified through `writeptr`, thus bypassing the protection provided by having the parameter declared as **const**.

Enumerations

An enumeration is a user-defined data type whose values consist of a set of named constants. In C++, you declare an enumeration with the **enum** keyword, just as in C.

In C, declarations of instances of an enumeration must include the **enum** keyword. In C++, an enumeration becomes a data type when you define it. Once defined, it is known by its identifier alone (the same as with any other type) and declarations can use the identifier name alone, without including the **enum** qualifier.

The following example demonstrates how a C++ program can reference an enumeration by using the identifier without the **enum** keyword:

```
// enum as a data type
#include <iostream.h>

enum color { red, orange, yellow, green, blue, violet };

void main()
{
    color myFavorite;

    myFavorite = blue;
}
```

Notice that the declaration of myFavorite uses only the identifier color; the **enum** keyword is unnecessary. Once color is defined as an enumeration, it becomes a new data type. (In later chapters, you'll see that classes have a similar property. When a class is defined, it becomes a new data type.)

Each element of an enumeration has an integer value, which, by default, is one greater than the value of the previous element. The first element has the value 0, unless you specify another value. You can also specify values for any subsequent element, and you can repeat values. For example:

```
enum color { red, orange, yellow, green, blue, violet );
// Values: 0, 1, 2, 3, 4, 5

enum day { sunday = 1, monday,
           tuesday, wednesday = 24,
           thursday, friday, saturday };
// Values: 1, 2, 3, 24, 25, 26, 27

enum direction { north = 1, south,
                 east = 1, west };
// Values: 1, 2, 1, 2
```

You can convert an enumeration into an integer. However, you cannot perform the reverse conversion unless you use a cast. For example:

```
// ENUM.CPP
enum color { red, orange, yellow, green, blue, violet };

void main()
{
    color myFavorite, yourFavorite;
    int i;

    myFavorite = blue;
    i = myFavorite;         // Legal; i = 4

 // yourFavorite = 5;       // Error: cannot convert
                            //     from int to color
    myFavorite = (color)4;  // Legal
}
```

Explicitly casting an integer into an enumeration is generally not safe. If the integer is outside the range of the enumeration or if the enumeration contains duplicate values, the result of the cast is undefined.

Overloaded Functions

Function overloading is a C++ feature that can make your programs more readable. For example, suppose you write one square root function that operates on integers, another square root function for floating-point variables, and yet another for doubles. In C, you have to give them three different names, even though they all perform essentially the same task. But in C++, you can name them all `square_root`. By doing so, you "overload" the name `square_root`; that is, you give it more than one meaning.

When you declare multiple functions with the same name, the compiler distinguishes them by comparing the number and type of their parameters. The following example overloads the `display_time` function to accept either a **tm** structure or a **time_t** value.

```
// OVERLOAD.CPP: Overloaded functions for different data formats
#include <iostream.h>
#include <time.h>

void display_time( const struct tm *tim )
{
    cout << "1. It is now " << asctime( tim );
}
```

```
void display_time( const time_t *tim )
{
    cout << "2. It is now " << ctime( tim );
}

void main()
{
    time_t tim = time( NULL );
    struct tm *ltim = localtime( &tim );

    display_time( ltim );
    display_time( &tim );
}
```

The example gets the current date and time by calling the **time** and **localtime** functions. Then it calls its own overloaded display_time function once for each of the formats. The compiler uses the type of the argument to choose the appropriate function for each call.

Depending on what time it is, the previous example prints something like this:

```
1. It is now Wed Jan 31 12:05:20 1992
2. It is now Wed Jan 31 12:05:20 1992
```

The different functions described by an overloaded name can have different return types. This makes it possible to have a max function that compares two integers and returns an integer, a max function that compares two floats and returns a float, and so on. However, the functions must also have different parameter lists. You cannot declare two functions that differ only in their return type. For example:

```
int search( char *key );
char *search( char *name );    // Error: has same parameter list
```

The compiler considers only the parameter lists when distinguishing functions with the same name.

You can also overload a name to describe functions that take different numbers of parameters but perform similar tasks. For example, consider the C run-time library functions for copying strings. The **strcpy** function copies a string from the source to the destination. The **strncpy** function copies a string, but stops copying when the source string terminates or after it copies a specified number of characters.

The following example replaces **strcpy** and **strncpy** with the single function name **string_copy**:

```
// An overloaded function
#include <iostream.h>
#include <string.h>

inline void string_copy( char *dest, const char *src )
{
    strcpy( dest, src );
}

inline void string_copy( char *dest, const char *src, int len )
{
    strncpy( dest, src, len );
}

static char stringa[20], stringb[20];

void main()
{
    string_copy( stringa, "That" );
    string_copy( stringb, "This is a string", 4 );
    cout << stringb << " and " << stringa;
}
```

This program has two functions named `string_copy`, which are distinguished by their different parameter lists. The first function takes two pointers to characters. The second function takes two pointers and an integer. The C++ compiler tells the two functions apart by examining their different parameter lists.

Default arguments can make one function's parameter list look like another's. Consider what happens if you give the second `string_copy` function a default value for the `len` parameter, as follows:

```
string_copy( char *dest, const char *src, int len = 10 );
```

In this case, the following function call is ambiguous:

```
string_copy( stringa, "That" );   // Error: ambiguous
```

This function call matches both the `string_copy` that takes two parameters and the one that takes three parameters with a default argument supplied. The compiler cannot tell which function should be called and gives an error.

You shouldn't overload a function name to describe completely unrelated functions. For example, consider the following pair:

```
void home();              // Move screen cursor to ( 0, 0 )
char *home( char *name ); // Look up person's home address
                          // and return it as a string
```

Because these functions perform totally different operations, they should have different names.

Linkage Specifications

This next feature is not so much a C++ extension to C as a way to let the two languages coexist. A "linkage specification" makes C functions accessible to a C++ program. Because there are differences in the way the two languages work, if you call functions originally compiled in C you must inform the C++ compiler of that fact.

The following example uses a linkage specification to tell the C++ compiler that the functions in MYLIB.H were compiled by a C compiler:

```
// Linkage specifications
#include <iostream.h>

extern "C"
{                        // The linkage specification
#include "mylib.h" // tells C++ that mylib functions
}                        // were compiled with C

void main()
{
    cout << myfunc();
}
```

The **extern "C"** statement says that everything in the scope of the braces is compiled by a C compiler. If you do not use the braces, the linkage specification applies only to the declaration that follows the **extern** statement on the same line.

You can also put the linkage specification in the header file that contains the prototypes for the C functions. You don't need to use the **extern "C"** statement when you're calling standard library functions because Microsoft includes the linkage specification in the standard C header files.

Sometimes, however, you need to use linkage specifications for other C header files. If you have a large library of custom C functions to include in your C++ program and you do not want to port them to C++, you must use a linkage specification. For example, perhaps you have libraries, but not the original source code.

Occasionally, you need to tell the C++ compiler to compile a function with C linkages. You would do this if the function was to be called from another function that was itself compiled with C linkage.

The following example illustrates a function that is to be compiled with C linkage because it is called from a C function:

```cpp
// LINKAGE.CPP: Linkage specifications
#include <iostream.h>
#include <stdlib.h>
#include <string.h>

// ------ Prototype for a C function
extern "C" int comp( const void *a, const void *b );

void main()
{
    // --------- Array of string pointers to be sorted
    static char *brothers[] = {
        "Frederick William",
        "Joseph Jensen",


        "Harry Alan",
        "Walter Elsworth",
        "Julian Paul"
    };
    // ---------- Sort the strings in alphabetical order
    qsort( brothers, 5, sizeof(char *), comp );
    // ---------- Display the brothers in sorted order
    for( int i = 0; i < 5; i++ )
        cout << brothers[i] << endl;
}

// ---------- A function compiled with C linkage
extern "C"
{
    int comp( const void *a, const void *b )
    {
        return strcmp( *(char **)a, *(char **)b );
    }
}
```

This program calls the C **qsort** function to sort an array of character pointers. The **qsort** function expects you to provide a function that compares two items. But **qsort** is a C function, so you must provide a C-compatible comp function. Because this program is a C++ program, you must tell the C++ compiler to use C linkage for this function alone. Both the prototype and the function definition have the **extern "C"** linkage specification.

References

This chapter explains how to use references, a new type of variable that C++ provides. References are primarily used to pass parameters to functions and return values back from functions. However, before you see how references are useful in those situations, you need to understand the properties of references. The first four sections of this chapter describe some characteristics of references, and the later sections explain the use of references with functions.

References as Aliases

You can think of a C++ reference as an alias for a variable—that is, an alternate name for that variable. When you initialize a reference, you associate it with a variable. The reference is permanently associated with that variable; you cannot change the reference to be an alias for a different variable later on.

The unary **&** operator identifies a reference, as illustrated below:

```
int actualint;
int &otherint = actualint;    // Reference declaration
```

These statements declare an integer named `actualint` and tell the compiler that `actualint` has another name, `otherint`. Now all operations on either name have the same result.

the following example shows how you can use a variable and a reference to that variable interchangeably:

```
// REFDEMO.CPP: The reference
#include <iostream.h>

void main()
{
    int actualint = 123;
    int &otherint = actualint;

    cout << actualint << endl;
    cout << otherint << endl;
    otherint++;
    cout << actualint << endl;
    cout << otherint << endl;
    actualint++;
    cout << actualint << endl;
    cout << otherint << endl;
}
```

The example shows that operations on `otherint` act upon `actualint`. The program displays the following output, showing that `otherint` and `actualint` are simply two names for the same item:

```
123
123
124
124
125
125
```

A reference is not a copy of the variable to which it refers. Instead, it is the same variable under a different name.

The following example displays the address of a variable and a reference to that variable:

```
// REFADDR.CPP: Addresses of references
#include <iostream.h>

void main()
{
    int actualint = 123;
    int &otherint = actualint;

    cout << &actualint << ' ' << &otherint << endl;
}
```

When you run the program, it prints the same address for both identifiers, the value of which depends on the configuration of your system.

Note that the unary operator **&** is used in two different ways in the example above. In the declaration of `otherint`, the **&** is part of the variable's type. The variable `otherint` has the type **int &**, or "reference to an **int**." This usage is unique to C++. In the **cout** statement, the **&** takes the address of the variable it is applied to. This usage is common to both C and C++.

Initializing a Reference

A reference cannot exist without a variable to refer to, and it cannot be manipulated as an independent entity. Therefore, you usually initialize a reference, explicitly giving it something to refer to, when you declare it.

There are some exceptions to this rule. You need not initialize a reference in the following situations:

- It is declared with **extern**, which means it has been initialized elsewhere.

- It is a member of a class, which means it is initialized in the class's constructor function. (For more information on class constructor functions, see Chapter 4, "Introduction to Classes.")

- It is declared as a parameter in a function declaration or definition, which means its value is established when the function is called.

- It is declared as the return type of a function, which means its value is established when the function returns something.

As you work through the examples in this and later chapters, note that a reference is initialized every time it is used, unless it meets one of these criteria.

References and Pointers: Similarities and Differences

You can also view references as pointers that you can use without the usual dereferencing notation. In the first example in this chapter, the reference `otherint` can be replaced with a constant pointer, as follows:

```
int actualint = 123;
int *const intptr = &actualint;   // Constant pointer
                                  // points to actualint
```

A declaration like this makes `*intptr` another way of referring to `actualint`. Consider the similarities between this and a reference declaration. Any assignments you make to `*intptr` affect `actualint`, and vice versa. As described earlier, a reference also has this property, but without requiring the *, or indirection operator. And because `*intptr` is a constant pointer, you cannot make it point to another integer once it's been initialized to `actualint`. Again, the same is true for a reference.

However, references cannot be manipulated as pointers can. With a pointer, you can distinguish between the pointer itself and the variable it points to by using the * operator. For example, `intptr` describes the pointer, while `*intptr` describes the integer being pointed to. Because you don't use a * with a reference, you can manipulate only the variable being referred to, not the reference itself.

As a result, there are a number of things that you cannot do to references themselves:

- Point to them
- Take the address of one
- Compare them
- Assign to them
- Do arithmetic with them
- Modify them

If you try to perform any of these operations on a reference, you instead act on the variable that the reference is associated with. For example, if you increment a reference, you actually increment what it refers to. If you take the address of a reference, you actually take the address of what it refers to.

Recall that with pointers, you can use the **const** keyword to declare constant pointers and pointers to constants. Similarly, you can declare a reference to a constant. For example:

```
int actualint = 123;
const int &otherint = actualint;    // Reference to constant int
```

This declaration makes `otherint` a read-only alias for `actualint`. You cannot make any modifications to `otherint`, only to `actualint`. The similarity to pointers does not go any further, however, because there is no reason to declare a constant reference:

```
int &const otherint = actualint;  // Warning: const is superfluous
```

This declaration is redundant because all references are constant by definition.

As mentioned earlier, the first sections of this chapter are intended to demonstrate the properties of references, but not their purpose. The previous examples notwithstanding, references should *not* be used merely to provide another name for a variable. The most common use of references is as function parameters.

References as Function Parameters

In C, there are two ways to pass a variable as a parameter to a function:

- Passing the variable itself. In this case, the function gets its own copy of the variable to work on. Creating a new copy of the variable on the stack can be time-consuming if, for example, the variable is a large structure.

- Passing a pointer to the variable. In this case, the function gets only the address of a variable, which it uses to access the caller's copy of the variable. This technique is much faster for large structures.

In C++, you have a third option: passing a reference to the variable. In this case, the function receives an alias to the caller's copy of the variable.

The following example illustrates all three techniques:

```cpp
// REFPARM.CPP: Reference parameters for reducing
//    overhead and eliminating pointer notation
#include <iostream.h>

// ---------- A big structure
struct bigone
{
    int serno;
    char text[1000];    // A lot of chars
} bo = { 123, "This is a BIG structure" };

// -- Three functions that have the structure as a parameter
void valfunc( bigone v1 );          // Call by value
void ptrfunc( const bigone *p1 );   // Call by pointer
void reffunc( const bigone &r1 );   // Call by reference

void main()
{
    valfunc( bo );    // Passing the variable itself
    ptrfunc( &bo );   // Passing the address of the variable
    reffunc( bo );    // Passing a reference to the variable
}

// ---- Pass by value
void valfunc( bigone v1 )
{
    cout << v1.serno << endl;
    cout << v1.text << endl;
}
// ---- Pass by pointer
void ptrfunc( const bigone *p1 )
{
    cout << p1->serno << endl;      // Pointer notation
    cout << p1->text << endl;
}

// ---- Pass by reference
void reffunc( const bigone &r1 )
{
    cout << r1.serno << endl;       // Reference notation
    cout << r1.text << endl;
}
```

The parameter r1 is a reference that is initialized with the variable bo when reffunc is called. Inside reffunc, the name r1 is an alias for bo. Unlike the previous examples of references, this reference has a different scope from that of the variable it refers to.

When you pass a reference as a parameter, the compiler actually passes the address of the caller's copy of the variable. Passing a reference is therefore just as efficient as passing a pointer, and, when passing large structures, far more efficient than passing by value. Also, the syntax for passing a reference to a variable is identical to that for passing the variable itself. No **&** is needed in the function call statement, and no **->** is needed when using the parameter within the function. Passing a reference thus combines the efficiency of passing a pointer and the syntactical cleanliness of passing by value.

When you pass a reference as a parameter, any modifications to the parameter are actually modifications to the caller's copy of the variable. This is significant because, unlike the syntax of passing a pointer, the syntax of passing a reference doesn't give any indication that such a modification is possible. For example:

```
valfunc( bo );    // Function can't modify bo
ptrfunc( &bo );   // & implies that function can modify bo
reffunc( bo );    // Same syntax as valfunc;
                  //     implies that function can't modify bo
```

The syntax for calling reffunc could make you think that the function cannot modify the variable you pass. In the case of reffunc, this assumption is correct. Because reffunc's parameter is a reference to a constant, its parameter is a read-only alias for the caller's copy of the variable. The reffunc function cannot modify the bo variable.

But you can also use an ordinary reference as a parameter instead of a reference to a constant. This allows the function to modify the caller's copy of the parameter, even though the function's calling syntax implies that it can't. For example:

```
// REFPARM2.CPP
// BAD TECHNIQUE: modifying a parameter through a reference
#include <iostream.h>

void func( int &parm );

void main()
{
    int a = 5;

    cout << a << endl;
    func( a );                 // function call looks harmless, but
    cout << a << endl;  // argument is unexpectedly modified
}

void func( int &parm )
{
    parm = 0;
}
```

Using references this way could be very confusing to someone reading your program.

For precisely this reason, you should use caution when passing references as function parameters. Don't assume that a reader of your program can tell whether a function modifies its parameters or not just by looking at the function's name. Without looking at the function's prototype, it is impossible to tell whether a function takes a reference or the variable itself. The function's calling syntax provides no clues.

To prevent such confusion, you should use the following guidelines when writing functions that take parameters too large to pass by value:

- If the function modifies the parameter, use a pointer.
- If the function doesn't modify the parameter, use a reference to a constant.

These rules are consistent with a common C-programming convention: When you explicitly take the address of a variable in order to pass it to a function, the function can modify the parameter. By following this convention, you make your C++ program more readable to C programmers. This is strictly a coding convention and cannot be enforced by the compiler. These rules do not make your programs correct or more efficient, but they do make them easier to read and understand.

Note that references are useful primarily when the parameter to be passed is a user-defined type, like a structure. Parameters of built-in types, such as characters or integers, can be efficiently passed by value.

References as Return Values

Besides passing parameters to a function, references can also be used to return values from a function. For example:

```
int mynum = 0;    // Global variable

int &num()
{
    return mynum;
}

void main()
{
    int i;

    i = num();
    num() = 5;    // mynum set to 5
}
```

In this example, the return value of the function num is a reference initialized with the global variable mynum. As a result, the expression num() acts as an alias for mynum. This means that a function call can appear on the receiving end of an assignment statement, as in the last line of the example.

You'll learn some more practical applications of this technique in Chapter 5, "Classes and Dynamic Memory Allocation," and Chapter 8, "Operator Overloading and Conversion Functions."

Passing a reference to a function and returning a reference from a function are the only two operations that you should perform on references themselves. Perform other operations on the object a reference refers to.

Summary

You will use references extensively when you build C++ classes, the subject of Part 2. As you do so, remember the following points about references:

- A reference is an alias for an actual variable.

- A reference must be initialized and cannot be changed.

- References are most useful when passing structures to a function and when returning values from a function.

Reference declarations are sometimes confused with the operation of taking the address of a variable, because both have the form **&***identifier*. To distinguish between these two uses of **&**, remember the following rules:

- When **&***identifier* is preceded by the name of a type, such as **int** or **char**, the **&** means "reference to" the type. This form of **&** occurs only in declarations, such as declaring the type of a reference variable, the type of a parameter, or a function's return type.

- When **&***identifier* is not preceded by the name of a type, the **&** means "address of" the variable. This form of **&** occurs most commonly when passing an argument to a function or when assigning a value to a pointer.

Note that there is no difference between *type* **&***identifier* and *type***&** *identifier*. Both syntax variations declare references.

Classes

Introduction to Classes

The most important feature of C++ is its support for user-defined types, through a mechanism called "classes." Classes are far more powerful than the user-defined types you can create in C. While an instance of a built-in type is called a variable, an instance of a class is called an "object," hence the phrase "object-oriented programming." Part 2 of this book describes classes, and Part 3 describes object-oriented programming.

This chapter covers the following topics:

- Declaring a class
- Using objects of a class
- Data members and member functions
- Constructors and destructors
- **const** objects and member functions
- Member objects
- Header and source files

Before explaining how to define a class in C++, let's consider one way you can create a new data type in C.

Creating a New Data Type in C

Suppose you're writing a C program that frequently manipulates dates. You might create a new data type to represent dates, using the following structure:

```
struct date
{
    int month;
    int day;
    int year;
};
```

This structure contains members for the month, day, and year.

To store a particular date, you can set the members of a date structure to the appropriate values:

```
struct date my_date;

my_date.month = 1;
my_date.day = 23;
my_date.year = 1985;
```

You cannot print a date by passing a date structure to **printf**. You must either print each member of the structure individually or write your own function to print the structure as a whole, as follows:

```
void display_date( struct date *dt )
{
    static char *name[] =
    {
        "zero", "January", "February", "March", "April", "May",
        "June", "July", "August", "September", "October",
        "November", "December"
    };

    printf( "%s %d, %d", name[dt->month], dt->day, dt->year );
}
```

This function prints the contents of a date structure, printing the month in string form, then the day and the year.

To perform other operations on dates, such as comparing two of them, you can compare the structure members individually, or you can write a function that accepts date structures as parameters and does the comparison for you.

When you define a structure type in C, you are defining a new data type. When you write functions to operate on those structures, you define the operations permitted on that data type.

This technique for implementing dates has some drawbacks:

- It does not guarantee that a `date` structure contains a valid date. You could accidentally set the members of a structure to represent a date like February 31, 1985, or you might have an uninitialized structure whose members represent the one-thousand-and-fifty-eighth day of the eighteenth month of a certain year. Any function that blindly uses such a variable generates nonsense results.

- Once you've used the `date` data type in your programs, you cannot easily change its implementation. Suppose later you become concerned about the amount of space that your `date` variables are taking up. You might decide to store both the month and day using a single integer, either by using bit fields or by saving only the day of the year (as a number from 1 to 365). Such a change would save two bytes per instance. To make this change, every program that uses the `date` data type must be rewritten. Every expression that accesses the month or day as separate integer members must be rewritten.

You could avoid these problems with more programming effort. For example, instead of setting the members of a `date` structure directly, you could use a function that tests the specified values for validity. And instead of reading the members of the structure directly, you could call functions that returned the value of a structure's members. Unfortunately, many programmers don't follow such practices when using a new data type in C. They find it more convenient to access the members of a `date` structure directly. As a result, their programs are more difficult to maintain.

Unlike C, C++ was designed to support the creation of user-defined data types. As a result, you don't have to expend as much programming effort to create a data type that is safe to use.

Creating a New Data Type in C++

With C++, you define both the data type and its operations at once, by declaring a "class." A class consists of data and functions that operate on that data.

Declaring the Class

A class declaration looks similar to a structure declaration, except that it has both functions and data as members, instead of just data. The following is a preliminary version of a class that describes a date:

```
// The Date class
#include <iostream.h>

// ------------ a Date class
class Date
{
public:
    Date( int mn, int dy, int yr );   // Constructor
    void display();                   // Function to print date
    ~Date();                          // Destructor
private:
    int month, day, year;             // Private data members
};
```

This class declaration is roughly equivalent to the combination of an ordinary structure declaration plus a set of function prototypes. It declares the following:

- The contents of each instance of Date: the integers month, day, and year. These are the class's "data members."

- The prototypes of three functions that you can use with Date: Date, ~Date, and display. These are the class's "member functions."

You supply the definitions of the member functions after the class declaration. Here are the definitions of Date's member functions:

```
// Some useful functions
inline int max( int a, int b )
{
    if( a > b ) return a;
    return b;
}

inline int min( int a, int b )
{
    if( a < b ) return a;
    return b;
}
```

```
// ---------- The constructor
Date::Date( int mn, int dy, int yr )
{
    static int length[] = { 0, 31, 28, 31, 30, 31, 30,
                               31, 31, 30, 31, 30, 31 };
    // Ignore leap years for simplicity
    month = max( 1, mn );
    month = min( month, 12 );

    day = max( 1, dy );
    day = min( day, length[month] );

    year = max( 1, yr );
}

// -------- Member function to print date
void Date::display()
{
    static char *name[] =
    {
        "zero", "January", "February", "March", "April", "May",
        "June", "July", "August", "September", "October",
        "November","December"
    };

    cout << name[month] << ' ' << day << ", " << year;
}

// ---------- The destructor
Date::~Date()
{
    // Do nothing
}
```

The display function looks familiar, but the Date and ~Date functions are new.
They are called the "constructor" and "destructor," respectively, and they are used to
create and destroy objects, or instances of a class. The constructor and the destructor
are described later in this chapter.

These are not all the member functions that a Date class needs, but they are
sufficient to demonstrate the basic syntax for writing a class. Later in this chapter,
we'll add more functionality to the class.

Here's a program that uses the rudimentary Date class:

```
// Program that demonstrates the Date class
void main()
{
    Date myDate( 3, 12, 1985 );       // Declare a Date
    Date yourDate( 23, 259, 1966 );   // Declare an invalid Date

    myDate.display();
    cout << endl;
    yourDate.display();
    cout << endl;
}
```

When you execute this program, notice that the variable yourDate contains a valid date, even though the variable was declared with nonsense values. The Date class permits only legitimate month and day combinations.

Using the Class

Once you've defined a class, you can declare one or more instances of that type, just as you do with built-in types like integers. As mentioned before, an instance of a class is called an "object" rather than a variable.

In the previous example, the **main** function declares two instances of the Date class called myDate and yourDate:

```
Date myDate( 3, 12, 1985 );       // Declare a Date
Date yourDate( 23, 259, 1966 );   // Declare an invalid Date
```

These are objects, and each one contains month, day, and year values.

The declaration of an object can contain a list of initializers in parentheses. The declarations of myDate and yourDate each contain three integer values as their initializers. These values are passed to the class's constructor, described later in "The Constructor."

Note the syntax for displaying the contents of Date objects. In C, you would pass each structure as an argument to a function, as follows:

```
// Displaying dates in C
display_date( &myDate );
display_date( &yourDate );
```

In C++, you invoke the member function for each object, using a syntax similar to that for accessing a structure's data member:

```
// Displaying dates in C++
myDate.display();
yourDate.display();
```

This syntax emphasizes the close relationship between the data type and the functions that act on it. It makes you think of the display operation as being part of the Date class.

However, this joining of the functions and the data appears only in the syntax. Each Date object does not contain its own copy of the display function's code. Each object contains only the data members.

Class Members

Now consider how the class declaration differs from a structure declaration in C:

```
class Date
{
public:
    Date( int mn, int dy, int yr );   // Constructor
    void display();                    // Function to print date
    ~Date();                           // Destructor
private:
    int month, day, year;              // Private data members
};
```

Like a structure declaration, it declares three data members: the integers month, day, and year. However, the class declaration differs from a structure declaration in several ways:

- It has the keywords **public** and **private**.
- It declares functions, such as display.
- It includes the constructor Date and the destructor ~Date.

Let's examine these differences one by one.

Class Member Visibility

The **private** and **public** labels in the class definition specify the visibility of the members that follow the labels. The mode invoked by a label continues until another label occurs or the class definition ends.

Private members can be accessed only by member functions. (They can also be accessed by friend classes and functions; for more information on friends, see Chapter 6, "More Features of Classes.") The private members define the internal workings of the class. They make up the class's "implementation."

Public members can be accessed by member functions, and by any other functions in the program as long as an instance of the class is in scope. The public members determine how the class appears to the rest of the program. They make up the class's "interface."

The Date class declares its three integer data members as private, which makes them visible only to functions within the class. If another function attempts to access one of these private data members, the compiler generates an error. For example, suppose you try to access the private data members of a Date object:

```
void main()
{
    int i;
    Date myDate( 3, 12, 1985 );

    i = myDate.month;     // Error: can't read private member
    myDate.day = 1;       // Error: can't modify private member
}
```

By contrast, the display function is public, which makes it visible to outside functions.

You can use the **private** and **public** labels as often as you want in a class definition, but most programmers group the private members together and the public members together. All class definitions begin with the private label as the default mode, but it improves readability to explicitly label all sections.

The Date class demonstrates a common C++ convention: Its public interface consists entirely of functions. You can view or modify a private data value only by calling a public member function designed for that purpose. This convention is discussed further in the section "Accessing Data Members."

Member Functions

The Date class has a member function named display. This function corresponds to the display_date function in C, which prints the contents of a date structure. However, notice the following differences.

First, consider the way the function is declared and defined. The function's prototype appears inside the declaration of `Date`, and when the function is defined, it is called `Date::display()`. This indicates that it is a member of the class and that its name has "class scope." You could declare another function named `display` outside the class, or in another class, without any conflict. The class name (combined with **::**, the scope resolution operator) prevents any confusion between the definitions.

You can also overload a member function, just as you can any other function in C++, as long as each version is distinguishable by its parameter list. All you have to do is declare each member function's prototype in the class declaration and prefix its name with the class name and **::** when defining it.

Now compare the implementation of the `display` member function with that of the corresponding function in C, `display_date`. The C function refers to `dt.month`, `dt.day`, and `dt.year`. In contrast, the C++ member function refers to `month`, `day`, and `year`; no object is specified. Those data members belong to the object that the function was called for. For example:

```
myDate.display();
yourDate.display();
```

The first time `display` is called, it uses the data members of `myDate`. The second time it's called, it uses the members of `yourDate`. A member function automatically uses the data members of the "current" object, the object to which it belongs.

You can also call a member function through a pointer to an object, using the **->** operator. For example:

```
Date myDate( 3, 12, 1985 );
Date *datePtr = &myDate;

datePtr->display();
```

This code declares a pointer to a `Date` object and calls `display` through that pointer.

You can even call a member function through a reference to an object. For example:

```
Date myDate( 3, 12, 1985 );
Date &otherDate = myDate;

otherDate.display();
```

This code calls `display` through the reference variable `otherDate`. Because `otherDate` is an alias for `myDate`, the contents of `myDate` are displayed.

These techniques for calling a member function work only if the function is declared **public**. If a member function is declared **private**, only other member functions within the same class can call it. For example:

```
class Date
{
public:
    void display();    // Public member function
    // ...
private:
    int daysSoFar();   // Private member function
    // ...
};

// --------- Display date in form "DDD YYYY"
void Date::display()
{

    cout << daysSoFar()        // Call private member function
         << " " << year;
}

 // -------- Compute number of days elapsed
int Date::daysSoFar()
{
    int total = 0;
    static int length[] = { 0, 31, 28, 31, 30, 31, 30,
                            31, 31, 30, 31, 30, 31 };

    for( int i = 1; i < month; i++ )
        total += length[i];

    total += day;
    return total;
}
```

Notice that display calls daysSoFar directly, without preceding it with an object name. A member function can use data members and other member functions without specifying an object. In either case, the "current" object is used implicitly.

The Constructor

Remember that the date structure in C had the drawback of not guaranteeing that it contained valid values. In C++, one way to ensure that objects always contain valid values is to write a constructor. A constructor is a special initialization function that is called automatically whenever an instance of your class is declared. This function prevents errors resulting from the use of uninitialized objects.

The constructor must have the same name as the class itself. For example, the constructor for the `Date` class is named `Date`.

Look at the implementation of the `Date` constructor:

```
Date::Date( int mn, int dy, int yr )
{
    static int length[] = { 0, 31, 28, 31, 30, 31, 30,
                               31, 31, 30, 31, 30, 31 };
    // Ignore leap years for simplicity
    month = max( 1, mn );
    month = min( month, 12 );

    day = max( 1, dy );
    day = min( day, length[month] );

    year = max( 1, year );
}
```

Not only does this function initialize the object's data members, it also checks that the specified values are valid; if a value is out of range, it substitutes the closest legal value. This is another way that a constructor can ensure that objects contain meaningful values.

Whenever an instance of a class comes into scope, the constructor is executed. Observe the declaration of `myDate` in the **main** function:

```
Date myDate( 3, 12, 1985 );
```

The syntax for declaring an object is similar to that for declaring an integer variable. You give the data type, in this case `Date`, and then the name of the object, `myDate`.

However, this object's declaration also contains an argument list in parentheses. These arguments are passed to the constructor function and are used to initialize the object. When you declare an integer variable, the program merely allocates enough memory to store the integer; it doesn't initialize that memory. When you declare an object, your constructor function initializes its data members.

You cannot specify a return type when declaring a constructor, not even **void**. Consequently, a constructor cannot contain a **return** statement. A constructor doesn't return a value; it creates an object.

You can declare more than one constructor for a class if each constructor has a different parameter list; that is, you can overload the constructors. This is useful if you want to initialize your objects in more than one way. This is demonstrated in the section "Accessing Data Members."

You aren't required to define any constructors when you define a class, but it is a good idea to do so. If you don't define any, the compiler automatically generates a do-nothing constructor that takes no parameters, just so you can declare instances of the class. However, this compiler-generated constructor doesn't initialize any data members, so any objects you declare are not any safer than C structures.

The Destructor

The destructor is the counterpart of the constructor. It is a member function that is called automatically when a class object goes out of scope. Its purpose is to perform any cleanup work necessary before an object is destroyed. The destructor's name is the class name with a tilde (~) as a prefix.

The Date class doesn't really need a destructor. One is included in this example simply to show its format.

Destructors are required for more complicated classes, where they're used to release dynamically allocated resources. For more information on such classes, see Chapter 5, "Classes and Dynamic Memory Allocation."

There is only one destructor for a class; you cannot overload it. A destructor takes no parameters and has no return value.

The Creation and Destruction of Objects

The following example defines a constructor and destructor that print messages, so you can see exactly when these functions are called:

```
// DEMO.CPP
#include <iostream.h>
#include <string.h>

class Demo
{
public:
    Demo( const char *nm );
    ~Demo();
private:
    char name[20];
};
```

```
Demo::Demo( const char *nm )
{
    strncpy( name, nm, 20 );
    cout << "Constructor called for " << name << endl;
}
Demo::~Demo()
{
    cout << "Destructor called for " << name << endl;
}

void func()
{
    Demo localFuncObject( "localFuncObject" );
    static Demo staticObject( "staticObject" );

    cout << "Inside func" << endl;
}

Demo globalObject( "globalObject" );

void main()
{
    Demo localMainObject( "localMainObject" );

    cout << "In main, before calling func\n";
    func();
    cout << "In main, after calling func\n";
}
```

The program prints the following:

```
Constructor called for globalObject
Constructor called for localMainObject
In main, before calling func
Constructor called for localFuncObject
Constructor called for staticObject
Inside func
Destructor called for localFuncObject
In main, after calling func
Destructor called for localMainObject
Destructor called for staticObject
Destructor called for globalObject
```

For local objects, the constructor is called when the object is declared and the destructor is called when the program exits the block in which the object is declared.

For global objects, the constructor is called when the program begins and the destructor is called when the program ends. For static objects, the constructor is called before the first entry to the function in which the static objects are declared and the destructor is called when the program ends.

Accessing Data Members

As it is currently defined, the Date class does not permit any access to its individual month, day, and year components. For example, you cannot read or modify the month value of a Date object. To remedy this, you can revise the Date class as follows:

```
class Date
{
public:
    Date( int mn, int dy, int yr );   // Constructor
                                      // Member functions:
    int getMonth();                   //    Get month
    int getDay();                     //    Get day
    int getYear();                    //    Get year
    void setMonth( int mn );          //    Set month
    void setDay( int dy );            //    Set day
    void setYear( int yr );           //    Set year
    void display();                   //    Print date
    ~Date();                          // Destructor
private:
    int month, day, year;             // Private data members
};
```

This version of Date includes member functions to read and modify the month, day, and year members. The function definitions are as follows:

```
inline int Date::getMonth()
{
    return month;
}

inline int Date::getDay()
{
    return day;
}

inline int Date::getYear()
{
    return year;
}
```

```
void Date::setMonth( int mn )
{
    month = max( 1, mn );
    month = min( month, 12 );
}

void Date::setDay( int dy )
{
    static int length[] = { 0, 31, 28, 31, 30, 31, 30,
                                31, 31, 30, 31, 30, 31 };
    day = max( 1, dy );
    day = min( day, length[month] );
}

void Date::setYear( int yr )
{
    year = max( 1, yr );
}
```

The various get functions simply return the value of the appropriate data member. However, the set functions do not simply assign a new value to a data member. These functions also check the validity of the specified value before assigning it. This is another way to ensure that Date objects contain valid values.

The following example uses these new member functions:

```
void main()
{
    int i;
    Date deadline( 3, 10, 1980 );

    i = deadline.getMonth();      // Read month value
    deadline.setMonth( 4 );       // Modify month value
    deadline.setMonth( deadline.getMonth() + 1 ); // Increment
}
```

Notice that the get functions are declared **inline** because they're so short. Because those functions have no function call overhead, calling them is as efficient as directly accessing public data members.

Member functions can also be declared inline without using the **inline** keyword. Instead, you can place the body of the function inside the class declaration, as follows:

```
class Date
{
public:
    Date( int mn, int dy, int yr );
    int getMonth() { return month; }   // Inline member functions
    int getDay() { return day; }
    int getYear() { return year; }
// etc....
};
```

This style of declaration has precisely the same effect as using the **inline** keyword with separate function definitions. You can use whichever style you find more readable.

Now that the class has member functions to set its values, you can change the way a Date object is constructed. You can overload constructors in the same way you overload other functions. The following example defines two versions of `Date`'s constructor, one that takes parameters and one that doesn't:

```
class Date
{
public:
    Date();      // Constructor with no parameters
    Date( int mn, int dy, int yr );  // Constructor with parameters
// etc....
};

Date::Date()
{
    month = day = year = 1;   // Initialize data members
}

Date::Date( int mn, int dy, int yr )
{
    setMonth( mn );
    setDay( dy );
    setYear( yr );
}

void main()
{
    Date myDate;       // Declare a date without arguments
    Date yourDate( 12, 25, 1990 );

    myDate.setMonth( 3 );   // Set values for myDate
    myDate.setDay( 12 );
    myDate.setYear( 1985 );
}
```

The declaration of `myDate` doesn't specify any initial values. As a result, the first constructor is used to create `myDate` and initialize it with the default value "January 1, 1." The values for `myDate` are specified later with the `set` functions. In contrast, the declaration of `yourDate` specifies three arguments. The second constructor is used to create `yourDate`, and this constructor calls the member functions to set the data members to the specified values. It is legal for a constructor to call member functions, as long as those functions don't read any uninitialized data members.

The first constructor in the example above is known as a "default constructor," because it can be called without arguments. If you define a default constructor, the compiler calls it automatically in certain situations; for more information, see "Member Objects," later in this chapter and "Arrays of Class Objects" in Chapter 6.

Access Functions vs. Public Data Members

Writing access functions might seem like a lot of needless work. You may argue that it's much simpler to declare the data members as public and manipulate them directly. After all, why call a setMonth and getMonth function when you could simply access the month member itself?

The advantages of access functions become apparent when we recall the example of the date structure defined in C. Access functions ensure that your objects never contain invalid values. You can always be sure that you can display the contents of a Date object without printing out nonsense.

More importantly, access functions let you change the implementation of your class easily. For example, remember the scenario in which you decide to encode the month and day within the bits of a single integer in order to save space. In C, you have to modify every program that uses date structures. This could involve thousands of lines of code.

In C++, however, all you have to rewrite are the class's member functions, which constitute far fewer lines. This change has no effect on any programs that use your Date class. They can still call getMonth and setMonth, just as they did before. The use of access functions instead of public members saves you a huge amount of rewriting.

By using member functions to control access to private data, you hide the representation of your class. Access functions let you change the implementation of a class without affecting any of the programs that use it. This convention is known as "encapsulation," which is one of the most important principles of object-oriented programming. Encapsulation is discussed in more detail in Chapter 9, "Fundamentals of Object-Oriented Design."

Returning a Reference

Occasionally, you may see a C++ program that declares member functions that act like public data members. Such functions return references to private data members. For example:

```
// BAD TECHNIQUE: Member function that returns a reference
class Date
{
public:
    Date( int mn, int dy, int yr );    // Constructor
    int &month();                       // Set/get month
    ~Date();                            // Destructor
```

```
private:
    int month_member,          // (_member appended to
        day_member,            //   distinguish names from
        year_member;           //   member functions)
};

int &Date::month()
{
    month_member = max( 1, month_member );
    month_member = min( month_member, 12 );
    return month_member;
}

// ...
```

The `month` member function returns a reference to the data member. This means that the function call expression `month()` can be treated as an alias for the private data member. For example:

```
// BAD TECHNIQUE: using member function that returns a reference
void main()
{
    int i;
    Date deadline( 3, 10, 1980 );

    i = deadline.month();    // Read month value
    deadline.month() = 4;    // Modify month value
    deadline.month()++;      // Increment
}
```

The member function behaves just like a data member. Consequently, the function call `deadline.month()` can appear on the left side of an assignment, in the same way that `deadline.month_member` could if the data member were public. You can even increment its value with the **++** operator.

You can assign an illegal value to `month_member` this way, but the `month` function performs range-checking to correct any such illegal values the next time it is called. As long as all of `Date`'s other member functions don't access the data member directly, but always use the `month` function instead, the `Date` class works correctly.

You should not use this technique for a variety of reasons. First, the syntax can be very confusing to people reading your program. Second, range checking is performed every time a data member is read, which is inefficient. Finally, and most importantly, this technique essentially makes the data member public. With this design, you cannot change the implementation of a private data member without rewriting all the programs that use the class. If you wanted to encode the month and day values within a single integer, you would have to change the member functions and rewrite all the programs that used `Date`.

To retain the benefits that member functions offer, you should always give your classes separate member functions to read and modify private data members.

const Objects and Member Functions

Just as you can use the **const** keyword when declaring a variable, you can also use it when declaring an object. Such a declaration means that the object is a constant, and none of its data members can be modified. For example:

```
const Date birthday( 7, 4, 1776 );
```

This declaration means that the value of `birthday` cannot be changed.

When you declare a variable as a constant, the compiler can usually identify operations that would modify it (such as assignment), and it can generate appropriate errors when it detects them. However, this is not true when you declare an object as a constant. The compiler can't tell whether a given member function might modify one of an object's data members, so it plays it safe and prevents you from calling any member functions for a **const** object.

However, some member functions don't modify any of an object's data members, so you should be able to call them for a **const** object. If you place the **const** keyword after a member function's parameter list, you declare the member function as a read-only function that doesn't modify its object. The following example declares some of the `Date` class's member functions as **const**:

```
class Date
{
public:
    Date( int mn, int dy, int yr );   // Constructor
                                      // Member functions:
    int getMonth() const;             //   Get month - read-only
    int getDay() const;               //   Get day - read-only
    int getYear() const;              //   Get year - read-only
    void setMonth( int mn );          //   Set month
    void setDay( int dy );            //   Set day
    void setYear( int yr );           //   Set year
    void display() const;             //   Print date - read-only
    ~Date();                          // Destructor
private:
    int month, day, year;             // Private data members
};

inline int Date::getMonth() const
{
    return month;
}
// etc...
```

The various `get` functions and the `display` function are all read-only functions. Note that the **const** keyword is used in both the declaration and the definition of each member function. These functions can be safely called for a constant object.

With the `Date` class modified in this way, the compiler can ensure that `birthday` is not modified:

```
int i;
const Date birthday( 7, 4, 1776 );

i = birthday.getYear();      // Legal
birthday.setYear( 1492 );    // Error: setYear not const
```

The compiler lets you call the **const** member function `getYear` for the `birthday` object, but not the function `setYear`, which is a non-**const** function.

A member function that is declared with **const** cannot modify any data members of the object, nor can it call any non-**const** member functions. If you declare any of the `set` functions as **const**, the compiler generates an error.

You should declare your member functions as **const** whenever possible. This allows people using your class to declare constant objects.

Member Objects

You can write a class that contains objects as members. This is known as "composition," the act of making a new class by using other classes as components. Suppose that you want a `PersonInfo` class that stores a person's name, address, and birthday. You can give that class a `Date` as a member, as follows:

```
class PersonInfo
{
public:
    // Public member functions...
private:
    char name[30];
    char address[60];
    Date birthday;              // Member object
};
```

This declaration specifies a private member named `birthday`, which is a `Date` object. Note that no arguments are specified in the declaration of `birthday`. However, this does not mean that the default constructor is called. The `birthday` object is not constructed until a `PersonInfo` object is constructed.

To call the constructor for a member object, you must specify a "member initializer." Place a colon after the parameter list of the containing class's constructor, and follow it with the name of the member and a list of arguments. For example, the constructor for `PersonInfo` is written as follows:

```
class PersonInfo
{
public:
    PersonInfo( char *nm, char *addr, int mn, int dy, int yr );
    // ...
private:
    // ...
};

PersonInfo::PersonInfo( char *nm, char *addr,
                        int mn, int dy, int yr )
    : birthday( mn, dy, yr ) // Member initializer
{
    strncpy( name, nm, 30 );
    strncpy( address, addr, 60 );
}
```

This syntax causes the `Date` class constructor to be invoked for the `birthday` member object, using the three arguments specified. The `Date` constructor is called first, so the `birthday` member is initialized before the `PersonInfo` constructor begins executing. If your class has more than one member object, you can specify a list of member initializers, separating them with commas.

Note To compile the PERSINFO.CPP sample file —which defines the `PersonInfo` class— using Visual C++ Standard Edition 4.0, you need to create a project workspace that contains both the PERSINFO.CPP and the DATE.CPP files. One way to do this is to first create a project workspace that contains the DATE.CPP file (using the procedure described in the first chapter), and then perform the following procedure:

1. From the Insert menu, choose the Files into Project command.

2. In the dialog box that appears, type the filename PERSINFO.CPP and choose OK.

The project workspace now contains both files. You do not need to explictly add header files to a project; they are included automatically by the **#include** statements in the source files.

Now when you build the program, both source files will be compiled and linked into the executable. To make use of the `PersonInfo` class from DATE.CPP's `main` function, simply add a **#include** statement specifying PERSINFO.H in the DATE.CPP file.

For more information about project workspaces, in Visual C++ Standard Edition 4.0, see the "Working with Projects" topic in Books Online. For more information about projects in Visual C++ 1.52, see "Using Projects" in the *Visual Workbench User's Guide* online.

If you don't use the member initializer syntax, the compiler implicitly calls the default constructor for the member object before constructing the containing object. You can then assign values to the member object using its access functions.

For example, because Date has a default constructor, you could write the PersonInfo constructor as follows:

```
PersonInfo::PersonInfo( char *nm, char *addr, int mn, int dy, int yr )
// Default constructor sets birthday to January 1, 1
{
    strncpy( name, nm, 30 );
    strncpy( address, addr, 60 );
    birthday.setMonth( mn );
    birthday.setDay( dy );
    birthday.setYear( yr );
}
```

If the member object's class doesn't define a default constructor, the compiler generates an error.

However, this is an inefficient technique because the value of birthday is set twice. First it is initialized to January 1, 1, by the default constructor, and then it is assigned the value specified by the member functions. In general, you should use member initializers to initialize your member objects, unless the default constructor performs all the initialization you need.

A member initializer is required when you have a constant member object. Because a person's birthday never changes, you can declare birthday with the **const** keyword. In this case, omitting the member initializer syntax is fatal. For example:

```
class PersonInfo
{
public:
    // ...
private:
    char name[30];
    char address[60];
    const Date birthday;        // Constant member object
};
PersonInfo::PersonInfo( char *nm, char *addr, int mn, int dy, int yr )
// Default constructor sets birthday to January 1, 1
{
    strncpy( name, nm, 30 );
    strncpy( address, addr, 60 );
    birthday.setMonth( mn );    // Error
    birthday.setDay( dy );      // Error
    birthday.setYear( yr );     // Error
}
```

Because birthday is a **const** object, you can't call any of its set member functions, because those are non-**const** functions. Thus, you have no way to change the value of birthday from the value that the default constructor initialized it to.

The same is true of any member declared **const**, even if it's a variable of a built-in type, like an integer. A **const** integer member cannot be assigned a value in the constructor; you must use a member initializer. For example:

```
class Count
{
public:
    Count( int i );     // Constructor
private:
    const int cnt;      // Constant integer member
};

Count( int i )
    : cnt( i )   // Member initializer for integer
{
}
```

Use a member initializer to initialize any **const** member, whether or not it's an object.

Using Header and Source Files

In C++, it's common practice to divide your source code into header and source files. You place the class declarations in the header files and place the definitions of the member functions in the source files. Header files usually have the filename extension .H, and source files have the filename extension .CPP. For example, here's a partial header file for the Date class:

```
// DATE.H
#if !defined( _DATE_H_ )

#define _DATE_H_

class Date
{
   Date();
   int getMonth() const;
   // ...
};

inline Date::getMonth() const
{
    return month;
}
// etc...

#endif  // _DATE_H_
```

Notice that this header file contains the definitions for inline member functions. The compiler must have access to the source code of an inline function in order to insert the code each time the function is called.

Also note that the header file uses the **#if** preprocessor directive and the **defined** preprocessor operator for conditional compilation. This prevents multiple inclusion of header files in a multimodule program.

Here's the beginning of a source file for the Date class:

```
// DATE.CPP
#include "date.h"

Date::Date()
{
    // ...
}
// etc...
```

Note that the source file includes its corresponding header file. See the DATE.H and DATE.CPP example files.

In general, you should use one header file and one source file for each class unless you are writing very small classes, or classes that are very closely related and should always be used together.

Roughly speaking, a header file describes a class's interface and a source file describes its implementation. This distinction is important when your classes may be used by other programmers. To use the Date class, for example, other programmers would simply include the header file DATE.H in their source files. Those programmers don't need to see how the member functions are implemented; all they need to see are the prototypes of the member functions. As long as they can link with DATE.OBJ when linking their program, they don't need to see DATE.CPP. If you rewrite DATE.CPP, you can simply recompile it to produce a new DATE.OBJ file; the other programmers don't need to change their code.

Unfortunately, it's necessary that some aspects of a class's implementation be revealed in the header file. The private members of a class are visible in the header file, even though they aren't accessible. Futhermore, if your class has inline member functions, their implementation is also visible. If you change the private members or inline functions of your class, those changes are reflected in the header file, and all the programmers who use that class must recompile their code with the new header file. However, they still don't have to rewrite any of their code, as long as the class's interface hasn't changed—that is, as long as you haven't changed the prototypes of the public member functions.

You should also consider whether your **#include** statements need to be in your header file or your source file. For example, if one of your class's member functions takes a **time_t** structure as a parameter, you have to place #include "time.h" in the header file. If the **time_t** structure is used only in the internal computations of a member function, and is not visible to someone calling the function, then you should place `#include "time.h"` in the source file instead. In the first case, the interface requires TIME.H, and in the second case, the implementation requires it. Don't place **#include** statements in your header files if placing them in the source file suffices.

By separating a class's interface and implementation, you make your classes as self-contained as possible, so they don't depend on each other's implementation details. This practice follows the principle of encapsulation, which is discussed in more detail in Chapter 9, "Fundamentals of Object-Oriented Design."

Classes and Dynamic Memory Allocation

C++ supports dynamic allocation and deallocation of objects from a pool of memory called the "free store." This chapter discusses the way objects are created, destroyed, copied, and converted to objects of other types.

Topics discussed include:

- The free store
- The assignment operator
- The **this** pointer
- The copy constructor
- Passing and returning objects
- Passing and returning references

Before continuing the discussion of classes, let's consider how you perform dynamic memory allocation in C++.

The Free Store

In C, the region of memory that is available at run time is called the heap. In C++, the region of available memory is known as the free store. The difference between the two lies in the functions you use to access this memory.

To request memory from the heap in C, you use the **malloc** function. For instance, you can dynamically allocate a `date` structure as follows:

```
struct date *dateptr;

dateptr = (struct date *)malloc( sizeof( struct date ) );
```

The **malloc** function allocates a block of memory large enough to hold a `date` structure and returns a pointer to it. The **malloc** function returns a void pointer, which you must cast to the appropriate type when you assign it to `dateptr`. You can now treat that block of memory as a `date` structure.

In C++, however, **malloc** is not appropriate for dynamically allocating a new instance of the Date class, because Date's constructor is supposed to be called whenever a new object is created. If you used **malloc** to create a new Date object, you would have a pointer to an uninitialized block of memory. You could then call member functions for an improperly constructed object, which would probably produce erroneous results. For example:

```
Date *datePtr;
int i;
datePtr = (Date *)malloc( sizeof( Date ) );
i = datePtr->getMonth();        // Returns undefined month value
```

If you use **malloc** to allocate objects, you lose the safety benefits that constructors provide. A better technique is to use the **new** operator.

The new Operator

As an alternative to **malloc**, C++ provides the **new** operator for allocating memory from the free store. The **malloc** function knows nothing about the type of the variable being allocated; it takes a size as a parameter and returns a void pointer. In contrast, the **new** operator knows the class of the object you're allocating, and it automatically calls the class's constructor to initialize the memory it allocates. Compare the previous example with the following:

```
Date *firstPtr, *secondPtr;
int i;
firstPtr = new Date;            // Default constructor called
i = firstPtr->getMonth();       // Returns 1 (default value)

secondPtr = new Date( 3, 15, 1985 );   // Constructor called
i = secondPtr->getMonth();             // Returns 3
```

The **new** operator calls the appropriate Date constructor, depending on whether you specify arguments or not. This ensures that any objects you allocate are properly constructed. You also don't have to use the **sizeof** operator to find the size of a Date object, because **new** can tell what size it is.

The **new** operator returns a pointer, but you don't have to cast it to a different type when you assign it to a pointer variable. The compiler checks that the type of the pointer matches that of the object being allocated and generates an error if they don't match. For example:

```
void *ptr;

ptr = new Date;    // Error; type mismatch
```

If **new** cannot allocate the memory requested, it returns 0. In C++, a null pointer has the value 0 instead of the value **NULL**.

The delete Operator

Just as the **malloc** function has the **free** function as its counterpart, the **new** operator has the **delete** operator as its counterpart. The **delete** operator deallocates blocks of memory, returning them to the free store for subsequent allocations.

The syntax for **delete** is simple:

```
Date *firstPtr;
int i;
firstPtr = new Date( 3, 15, 1985 ); // Constructor called
i = firstPtr->getMonth();           // Returns 3

delete firstPtr;                 // Destructor called, memory freed
```

The **delete** operator automatically calls the destructor for the object before it deallocates the memory. Because the Date class's destructor doesn't do anything, this feature is not demonstrated in this example.

You can only apply **delete** to pointers that were returned by **new**, and you can only delete them once. Deleting a pointer not obtained from **new** or deleting a pointer twice causes your program to behave strangely, and possibly to crash. It is your responsibility to guard against these errors; the compiler cannot detect them. You can, however, delete a null pointer (a pointer with value 0) without any adverse effects.

The Free Store and Built-in Types

The **new** and **delete** operators can be used not only with classes that you've defined, but also with built-in types such as integers and characters. For example:

```
int *ip;

ip = new int;   // Allocate an integer
// use ip
delete ip;
```

You can also allocate arrays whose size is determined at run time:

```
int length;
char *cp;

// Assign value to length, depending on user input
cp = new char[length];        // Allocate an array of chars
// Use cp
delete [] cp;
```

Notice the syntax for declaring an array: You place the array size within brackets after the name of the type. Also note the syntax for deleting an array: You place an empty pair of brackets before the name of the pointer. The compiler ignores any number you place inside the brackets.

You can even allocate multidimensional arrays with **new**, as long as all of the array dimensions except the first are constants. For example:

```
int (*matrix)[10];
int size;

// Assign value to size, depending on user input
matrix = new int[size][10];     // Allocate a 2-D array
// Use matrix
delete [] matrix;
```

Dynamic allocation of arrays of objects, as opposed to arrays of built-in types, is discussed in Chapter 6, "More Features of Classes."

Classes with Pointer Members

You can use the **new** and **delete** operators from within the member functions of a class. Suppose you wanted to write a String class, where each object contains a character string. It's inappropriate to store the strings as arrays, because you don't know how long they'll be. Instead, you can give each object a character pointer as a member and dynamically allocate an appropriate amount of memory for each object. For example:

```
// See STRNG.H and STRNG.CPP for final versions of this example
#include <iostream.h>
#include <string.h>

// ------- A string class
class String
{
public:
    String();
    String( const char *s );
    String( char c, int n );
```

```cpp
      void set( int index, char newchar );
      char get( int index ) const;
      int getLength() const { return length; }
      void display() const { cout << buf; }
      ~String();
private:
      int length;
      char *buf;
};

// Default constructor
String::String()
{
     buf = 0;
     length = 0;
}

// ---------- Constructor that takes a const char *
String::String( const char *s )
{
     length = strlen( s );
   ' buf = new char[length + 1];
     strcpy( buf, s );
}

// ---------- Constructor that takes a char and an int
String::String( char c, int n )
{
     length = n;
     buf = new char[length + 1];
     memset( buf, c, length );
     buf[length] = '\0'; }

// ---------- Set a character in a String
void String::set( int index, char newchar )
{
     if( (index > 0) && (index <= length) )
     buf[index - 1] = newchar;
}
// ---------- Get a character in a String
char String::get( int index ) const
{
     if( (index > 0) && (index <= length) )
     return buf[index - 1];
     else
     return 0;
}
// ---------- Destructor for a String
String::~String()
{
     delete [] buf;    // Works even for empty String; delete 0 is safe
}
```

```
main()
{
    String myString( "here's my string" );
    myString.set( 1, 'H' );
}
```

The `String` constructor that takes a character pointer uses the **new** operator to allocate a buffer to contain the string. It then copies the contents of the string into the buffer. As a result, a `String` object is not a contiguous block of memory the way a structure variable is. Each `String` object consists of two blocks of memory, one that contains `length` and `buf`, and another that stores the characters themselves.

If you call **sizeof** to find the size of a `String` object, you get only the size of the block containing the integer and the pointer. However, different `String` objects may have character buffers of different lengths.

In fact, you can write a member function that changes the length of a `String` object's character buffer. For example:

```
void String::append( const char *addition )
{
    char *temp;

    length += strlen( addition );
    temp = new char[length + 1];      // Allocate new buffer
    strcpy( temp, buf );              // Copy contents of old buffer
    strcat( temp, addition );         // Append new string
    delete [] buf;                    // Deallocate old buffer
    buf = temp;
}
```

This function appends a new string to the contents of an existing `String` object. For example:

```
String myString( "here's my string" );

myString.append( " and here's more of it" );
// myString now holds "here's my string and here's more of it"
```

The String object defined above is thus dynamically resizable. All the details of the resizing are handled by the member functions.

The String class is an example of a class that requires a destructor. When a String object goes out of scope, the block of memory containing length and buf is deallocated automatically. However, the character buffer was allocated with **new**, so it must be deallocated explicitly. As a result, the String class defines a destructor that uses the **delete** operator to deallocate the character buffer. If the class didn't have a destructor, the character buffers would never be deallocated and the program might eventually run out of memory.

The String class has potential problems, however. Suppose you added the following code to the **main** function in this example:

```
String yourString( "here's your string" );
yourString = myString;
```

The program constructs a String object named yourString and then assigns the contents of myString to it. This looks harmless enough, but it actually causes problems.

When you assign one object to another, the compiler performs a memberwise assignment; that is, it does the equivalent of the following:

```
// Hypothetical equivalent of yourString = myString
yourString.length = myString.length;
yourString.buf = myString.buf;
```

The assignment of the length member is no problem. However, the buf member is a pointer. The result of the pointer assignment is that yourString.buf and myString.buf point to the same location in memory. The two objects share the same character buffer. This is illustrated in Figure 5.1.

Figure 5.1 Default Assignment Behavior

Before assignment

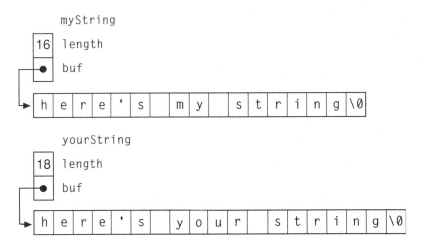

Result of yourString = myString **using default assignment behavior:**

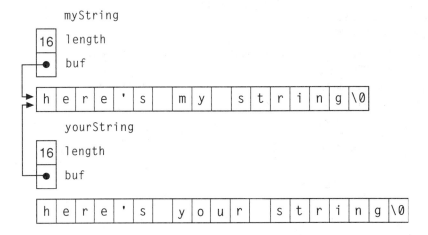

This means that any modifications to one of the String objects affects both of them. If you call myString.set(), you modify yourString as well. This behavior probably isn't what you desired.

More serious problems arise when the objects go out of scope. When the `String` class's destructor is called for `myString`, it deletes the object's `buf` pointer, deallocating the memory that it points to. Then the destructor is called again for `yourString`, and it deletes that object's `buf` pointer. But both `buf` members have the same value, which means the pointer is deleted twice. This can cause unpredictable results. Furthermore, the original buffer in `yourString`, containing "here's your string," is lost. That block of memory is never deleted.

These problems occur for any class that has pointer members and allocates memory from the free store. The compiler's default behavior for assigning one object to another is unsatisfactory for such classes. The solution is to replace the compiler's default behavior by writing a special function to perform the assignment, called the "assignment operator."

The Assignment Operator

As described in Chapter 2, "C++ Enhancements to C," in C++ you can overload a function name so that it applies to more than one function. Similarly, you can overload the assignment operator (the = sign) to have more than one meaning; you can specify what happens when it is applied to instances of a particular class. This is known as "operator overloading." Chapter 8, "Operator Overloading and Conversion Functions," explains operator overloading in greater detail.

To redefine the meaning of the assignment operator for a class, you write a member function with the name **operator=**. If your class defines such a function, the compiler calls it whenever one object is assigned to another. The compiler interprets an assignment statement like this:

```
yourstring = mystring;
```

as a function call that looks like this:

```
yourstring.operator=( mystring );
```

In fact, you can explicitly use the second syntax to perform assignments; however, you should use the first syntax because it is more readable.

The assignment operator for String can be written as follows:

```
// Class Assignment
#include <iostream.h>
#include <string.h>

class String
{
public:
    String();
    String( const char *s );
    String( char c, int n );
    void operator=( const String &other );
// etc...
};

// ----------- Assignment operator
void String::operator=( const String &other )
{
    length = other.length;
    delete [] buf;
    buf = new char[length + 1];
    strcpy( buf, other.buf );
}
```

The assignment operator takes a reference to an object as its parameter. (Note that a reference to a constant is used, indicating that the function doesn't modify the object.) To perform the assignment, the function first copies the length data member. Next, it deletes the receiving object's buf pointer, returning that block of memory to the free store (this is safe even for an uninitialized string, because deleting a 0 pointer has no effect). Then the function allocates a new buffer and copies the other buffer's contents into it. This is illustrated in Figure 5.2.

Figure 5.2   Correct Assignment Behavior

Result of `yourString = myString` **after assignment operator has been defined:**

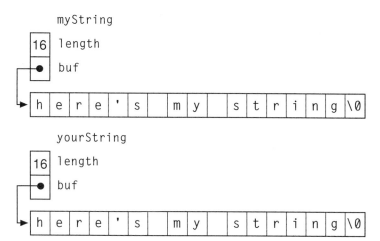

Here's a program that uses the new `String` class with its assignment operator:

```
main()
{
    String myString( "here's my string" );
    myString.display();
    cout << endl;

    String yourString( "here's your string" );
    yourString.display();
    cout << endl;

    yourString = myString;
    yourString.display();
    cout << endl;
}
```

This program prints the following messages:

```
here's my string
here's your string
here's my string
```

What if a programmer using the `String` class accidentally assigns an object to itself? For instance:

```
myString = myString;   // Self-assignment
```

Few people would write such a statement, but self-assignment can take other forms. For instance:

```
String *stringPtr = &myString;

// Later...
myString = *stringPtr;     // Inconspicuous self-assignment
```

What happens during such an assignment? The **operator=** defined above first deletes `myString`'s buffer and allocates a new buffer. Then it copies the contents of `myString`'s newly allocated buffer into itself. This causes unpredictable behavior in your program.

In order for the **operator=** function to work safely in all cases, it must check against self-assignment. This requires the use of the **this** pointer.

The this Pointer

The **this** pointer is a special pointer that is accessible to member functions. The **this** pointer points to the object for which the member function is called. (There is no **this** pointer accessible to static member functions. Static member functions are described in Chapter 6, "More Features of Classes.")

When you call a member function for an object, the compiler assigns the address of the object to the **this** pointer and then calls the function. Every time a member function accesses one of the class's data members, it is implicitly using the **this** pointer.

For example, consider the following C++ code fragment, describing a member function definition and function call:

```
void Date::setMonth( int mn )
{
    month = mn;
}


...
// Member function call
myDate.setMonth( 3 );
```

This is roughly equivalent to the following C fragment:

```
// C equivalent of C++ member function
void Date_setMonth( Date *const this, int mn )
{
    this->month = mn;
}
...

// Function call
Date_setMonth( &myDate, 3 );
```

Notice that the type of **this** is Date * for member functions of Date; the type is different for member functions of other classes.

When you write a member function, it is legal to explicitly use the **this** pointer when accessing any members, though it is unnecessary. You can also use the expression ***this** to refer to the object for which the member function was called. Thus, in the following example, the three statements are equivalent:

```
void Date::month_display()
{
    cout << month;          // These three statements
    cout << this->month;    //     do the same thing
    cout << (*this).month;
}
```

A member object can use the **this** pointer to test whether an object passed as a parameter is the same object that the member function is called for. For example, the **operator=** function for the String class can be rewritten as follows:

```
void String::operator=( const String &other )
{
    if( &other == this )
        return;
    delete [] buf;
    length = other.length;
    buf = new char[length + 1];
    strcpy( buf, other.buf );
}
```

The function tests whether the address of the other object is equal to the value of the **this** pointer. If so, a self-assignment is being attempted, so the function exits without doing anything. Otherwise, it performs the assignment as usual.

Using *this in a Return Statement

The **this** pointer can also be used in the **return** statement of a member function. In both C and C++, an assignment statement can be treated as an expression, which has the value of what was being assigned. For example, the statement

```
i = 3;
```

is an expression with the value 3.

One result of this is that you can chain together multiple assignment statements:

```
a = b = c;
```

The assignment operator is right associative, so the expression is evaluated from right to left. This means the expression is equivalent to the following:

```
a = (b = c);
```

To make your overloaded class assignments work this way, you must make the assignment function return the result of the assignment. You want the assignment operator to return the object to which it belongs. You get the address of the object from the **this** pointer.

Returning ***this** involves a simple modification to the assignment operator (in the **operator=** function):

```
String &String::operator=( const String &other )
{
    if( &other == this )
        return *this;
    delete [] buf;
    length = other.length;
    buf = new char[length + 1];
    strcpy( buf, other.buf );
    return *this;
}
```

With this version of the **operator=** function, you can chain together assignments of String objects:

```
herString = yourString = myString;
```

Note that the function returns a reference to a String. This is more efficient than returning an actual String object; for more information on returning objects from functions, see the section "The Copy Constructor."

The practice of returning ***this** also explains how the chained `cout` statements used in previous examples work. You have seen many statements similar to the following:

```
cout << a << b << c;
```

The left-shift operator is left-associative, so this expression is evaluated from left to right. The overloaded left-shift operator returns ***this**, which is the `cout` object, so each variable is printed successively.

Bad Uses of the this Pointer

The **this** pointer is a **const** pointer, so a member function cannot change the pointer's value to make it point to something else. In early versions of C++, the **this** pointer was not a **const** pointer. This made it possible for a programmer to make assignments to the **this** pointer in order to perform customized memory allocation. For example:

```
// BAD TECHNIQUE: assignment to this
class foo
{
public:
    foo() { this = my_alloc( sizeof( foo ) ); }
   ~foo() { my_dealloc( this ); this = 0; }
};
```

This type of special processing is not allowed in the current version of C++. If you need customized memory allocation, you can write your own versions of **new** and **delete**. For more information, see the section "Class-Specific new and delete Operators" in Chapter 6.

Early versions of C++ also let you examine the **this** pointer to distinguish between objects allocated on the stack and those allocated with the free store. On entry to a constructor, the **this** pointer had a value of 0 if the constructor was being called for an object allocated with **new** and had a nonzero value otherwise. This made it possible for you to perform different processing for dynamically allocated objects. This behavior is not supported in the current version of C++.

Assignment vs. Initialization

Consider the following two code fragments:

```
int i;

i = 3;
```

and

```
int i = 3;
```

In C, these two fragments have the same effect and can be regarded as the same. In C++, however, they are very different. In the first example, the integer i is *assigned* a value. In the second example, it is *initialized* with a value.

The differences are as follows:

- An assignment occurs when the value of an existing object is changed; an object can be assigned new values many times.

- An initialization occurs when an object is given an initial value when it is first declared; an object can be initialized only once.

One way to illustrate the difference is to consider variables declared as **const**. A constant variable can only be initialized; it cannot be assigned a new value. (Similarly, references are initialized with a variable, but they cannot be assigned a new variable.)

This distinction becomes important when using objects. Consider the previous examples with the integers replaced by String objects. Here's an assignment:

```
String myString( "this is my string" );
String yourString;

yourString = myString;  // Assign one String the value of another
```

Here's an initialization:

```
String myString( "this is my string" );
String yourString = myString;  // Initialize one String with another
```

As previously described, the assignment statement causes the compiler to invoke the **operator=** function defined for the class. However, the initialization does not invoke the same function. The **operator=** function can only be called for an object that has already been constructed. In the above example, yourString is being constructed at the same time that it receives the value of another object. To construct an object in this way, the compiler invokes a special constructor called the "copy constructor."

The Copy Constructor

A copy constructor is a constructor that takes an object of the same type as an argument. It is invoked whenever you initialize an object with the value of another. It can be invoked with the = sign, as in the example in the previous section, "Assignment vs. Initialization," or with function-call syntax. For example, the initialization in the example above could be rewritten with the following syntax:

```
String yourString( myString );
```

This follows the traditional syntax for calling a constructor.

The way the String class is currently written, the compiler executes the previous statement by initializing each member of yourString with the values of the members of myString. Just as with the default behavior during assignment, this is generally undesirable when the class contains pointers as members. The result of the previous initialization is to give yourString and myString the same character buffer, which can cause errors when the destructor destroys the objects.

The solution is to write your own copy constructor. The copy constructor for the String class can be written as follows:

```
#include <iostream.h>
#include <string.h>

// ------- string class
class String
{
public:
    String();
    String( const char *s );
    String( char c, int n );
    String( const String &other );    // Copy constructor
// etc...
};

// ----------- Copy constructor
String::String( const String &other )
{
    length = other.length;
    buf = new char[length + 1];
    strcpy( buf, other.buf );
}
```

The implementation of the copy constructor is similar to that of the assignment operator in that it allocates a new character buffer for the object being created. Note that the copy constructor actually takes a reference to an object, instead of an object itself, as a parameter.

In general, there are only a few differences between copy constructors and assignment operators:

- An assignment operator acts on an existing object, while a copy constructor creates a new one. As a result, an assignment operator may have to delete the memory originally allocated for the receiving object.

- An assignment operator must check against self-assignment. The copy constructor doesn't have to, because self-initialization is impossible.

- To permit chained assignments, an assignment operator must return ***this**. Because it is a constructor, a copy constructor has no return value.

Passing and Returning Objects

There are two other situations besides ordinary declarations in which the copy constructor may be called:

- When a function takes an object as a parameter.

- When a function returns an object.

The following example shows a function that takes an object as a parameter:

```
// Function that takes a String parameter
void consume( String parm )
{
    // Use the parm object
}

void main()
{
    String myString( "here's my string" );

    consume( myString );
}
```

The function consume takes a String object passed by value. That means that the function gets its own private copy of the object.

The function's parameter is initialized with the object that is passed as an argument. The compiler implicitly calls the copy constructor to perform this initialization. It does the equivalent of the following:

```
// Hypothetical initialization of parameter
String parm( myString );   // Call copy constructor
```

Consider what happens if you don't define a copy constructor to handle initialization. As a result of the compiler's default initialization, the function's copy of the object has the same character buffer as the caller's copy; any operations on parm's buffer also modify myString's buffer. More importantly, the parameter has local scope, so the destructor is called to destroy it when the function finishes executing. That means that myString has a pointer to deleted memory, which makes it unsafe to use after the function is done.

The following example shows a function that returns an object:

```
// Function that returns a String
String emit()
{
    String retValue( "here's a return value" );

    return retValue;
}

void main()
{
    String yourString;

    yourString = emit();
}
```

The function emit returns a String object. The compiler calls the copy constructor to initialize a hidden temporary object in the caller's scope, using the object specified in the function's **return** statement. This hidden temporary object is then used as the right-hand side of the assignment statement. That is, the compiler performs the equivalent of the following:

```
// Hypothetical initialization of return value
String temp( retValue ); // Call copy constructor
yourString = temp;       // Assignment of temp object
```

Once again, a copy constructor is needed. Otherwise, the temporary object shares the same character buffer as retValue, which is deleted when the function finishes executing, and the subsequent assignment to yourString is not guaranteed to work.

As a rule, you should always define both a copy constructor and an assignment operator whenever you write a class that contains pointer members and allocates memory from the free store.

Passing and Returning References to Objects

There is some overhead involved in calling the copy constructor every time an object is passed by value to a function. However, you can duplicate the effect of passing the parameter by value, while avoiding the expense of the constructor call, by passing a reference to a constant object. For example:

```
void consume( const String &parm )
{
    // Use the parm object
}

void main()
{
    String myString( "here's my string" );

    consume( myString );
}
```

The copy constructor is not called when a parameter is passed this way, because a new object is not being constructed. Instead, a reference is initialized with the object being passed. The compiler performs the equivalent of the following:

```
// Hypothetical initialization of reference parameter
const String &parm = myString;    // Initialize reference
```

As a result, the function uses the same object as the caller.

Notice that the **const** keyword is used. Because a reference to a constant is passed, the function cannot modify the parameter, so the caller is guaranteed that the object remains safe. Only **const** member functions (that is, read-only member functions) can be invoked on the object.

Note that the copy constructor itself takes a reference to an object, rather than an object, as its parameter. If the copy constructor took an object itself as a parameter, it would have to call itself in order to initialize the parameter. This would cause an infinite recursion.

Returning a reference from a function can also be more efficient than returning an object. Recall the example of the **operator=** function:

```
String &String::operator=( const String &other )
{
    //...
    return *this;
}
```

```
void main()
{
    String myString( "here's my string" );
    String yourString, herString;

    herString = yourString = myString;
}
```

The copy constructor is not called when the function returns, because a temporary object is not being created: Only a temporary reference is created. When the herString object receives the value of the yourString = myString assignment statement, the compiler performs the equivalent of the following:

```
// Hypothetical initialization of reference return value
String &tempRef = yourString;    // Initialize reference
                                 // NOTE: yourString == *this
herString = tempRef;      // Assignment of temp reference
                          // Equivalent to herString = yourString
```

However, you must use caution when returning a reference to objects or variables other than ***this**. The rules for returning references are similar to those for returning pointers. You cannot return a pointer to an automatic variable. For example:

```
// BAD TECHNIQUE: returning pointer to automatic variable
int *emitPtr()
{
    int i;

    return &i;
}
```

The integer i is an automatic variable, so it goes out of scope at the end of the function. That means the function returns a pointer to an integer that no longer exists. It is unsafe for the calling program to use such a pointer.

The same restriction applies to references:

```
// BAD TECHNIQUE: returning reference to automatic variable
int &emitRef()
{
    int i;

    return i;
}
```

It is safe, however, to return a reference or a pointer to a variable that has been dynamically allocated. Dynamically allocated objects remain in existence until they are deallocated, so references and pointers to them remain valid even after the function has exited. You can also safely return references or pointers to static or global variables.

More Features of Classes

This chapter describes the following additional features of classes:

- Static members
- Friend classes and functions
- Creating arrays of objects
- The **set_new_handler** function
- Writing your own **new** and **delete** operators

Static Members

Suppose you write a class `SavingsAccount` to represent savings accounts at a bank. Each object represents a particular customer's account and has data members storing the customer's name and the account's current balance. The class also has a member function to increase an account's balance by the interest earned in one day.

In such a class, how would you represent the daily interest rate? The interest rate may change, so it has to be a variable instead of a constant. You could make it a member of the class, but then each object would have its own copy. This is not only a waste of space, but it also requires you to update every single object each time the interest rate changes, which is inefficient and could lead to inconsistencies.

You could make the interest rate a global variable, but then every function would be able to modify its value. What you want is a kind of global variable for an individual class. For such situations, C++ lets you declare a member of a class to be **static**.

Static Data Members

When a data member is declared **static**, only one copy of it is allocated, no matter how many instances of the class are declared. However, it can be treated like an ordinary data member by the class's member functions. If it is declared **private**, only the member functions can access it. For example, here's a declaration of a SavingsAccount class that contains a static member called currentRate:

```
class SavingsAccount
{
public:
    SavingsAccount();
    void earnInterest() { total += currentRate * total; }
    //...
private:
    char name[30];
    double total;
    static double currentRate;
    //...
};
```

Only one copy of currentRate exists, and it is accessible to all SavingsAccount objects. Whenever the earnInterest member is called for any SavingsAccount object, the same value of currentRate is used. This is illustrated in Figure 6.1.

Figure 6.1 A Static Data Member

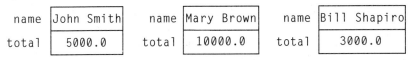

You can declare a static member **public**, making it visible to the rest of the program. You can then access it as if it were an ordinary data member of an object.

For example, if currentRate were a public member, you could access it as follows:

```
// If currentRate were a public member
void main()
{
    SavingsAccount myAccount;
    myAccount.currentRate = 0.000154;
}
```

However, this syntax is misleading, because it implies that only the interest rate of myAccount is being modified, when in fact the interest rate of all SavingsAccount objects is being modified. A better way of referring to a static member is to prefix its name with the class name and the scope resolution operator. For example:

```
// If currentRate were a public member
void main()
{
    SavingsAccount::currentRate = 0.000154;
}
```

This syntax reflects the fact that the value being modified applies to the class as a whole, rather than an individual object. You can use this syntax even if you haven't declared any SavingsAccount objects; a static data member exists even if no instances of the class are declared.

You cannot initialize a static data member from within a constructor of the class, because the constructor may be called many times and a variable can be initialized only once. A static data member must be initialized at file scope, as if it were a global variable. The access specifier for a static data member is not in effect during initialization; private static members are initialized in the same way as public ones. For example:

```
#include "savings.h"

// Initialize private static member at file scope
double SavingsAccount::currentRate = 0.0001;

    SavingsAccount::SavingsAccount()
{
    // ...
}
// etc....
```

Notice that the initialization is not placed in a header file, because that file may be included more than once in a program. The initialization is placed in the source module that contains the definitions of the class's member functions. Also note that the type of the static member is specified, because it is an initialization rather than an assignment. The static member is being declared at that point, not inside the class.

Static Member Functions

If you have a member function that accesses only the static data members of a class, you can declare the function **static** as well. For example:

```
// See SAVINGS.H and SAVINGS.CPP for final versions
//      of this example
class SavingsAccount
{
public:
    SavingsAccount();
    void earnInterest() { total += currentRate * total; }
    static void setInterest( double newValue )
        { currentRate = newValue; }
    //...
private:
    char name[30];
    double total;
    static double currentRate;
    //...
};
```

Static member functions can be called using the same syntax as that used for accessing static data members. That is:

```
// Calling a static member function
void main()
{
    SavingsAccount myAccount;

    myAccount.setInterest( 0.000154 );
    SavingsAccount::setInterest( 0.000154 );
}
```

Because a static member function doesn't act on any particular instance of the class, it has no **this** pointer. Consequently, a static member function cannot access any of the class's nonstatic data members or call any nonstatic member functions, as doing so would mean implicitly using the **this** pointer. For example, the function setInterest cannot access the total data member; if it could, which object's value of total would it use?

Static members are useful for implementing common resources that all the objects need, or maintaining state information about the objects. One use of static members is to count how many instances of a class exist at any particular moment. This is done by incrementing a static member each time an object is created and decrementing it each time an object is destroyed. For example:

```
class Airplane
{
public:
    Airplane() { count++; }
    static int howMany() { return count; }
    ~Airplane() { count--; }
private:
    static int count;
};

// Initialize static member at file scope
int Airplane::count = 0;
```

By calling `howMany`, you can get the number of `Airplane` objects that exist at any particular time.

Friends

As mentioned in Chapter 4, "Introduction to Classes," you should declare your class's data members **private**, so that they're inaccessible to functions outside of the class. This lets you change the implementation of a class without affecting the programs that use the class.

Sometimes, however, you may find that two or more classes must work together very closely—so closely that it's inefficient for them to use each other's access functions. You may want one class to have direct access to another class's private data. You can permit this by using the **friend** keyword.

Friend Classes

In the following example, the class `YourClass` declares that the `YourOtherClass` class is a friend. This permits member functions of `YourOtherClass` to directly read or modify the private data of `YourClass`:

```
class YourClass
{
friend class YourOtherClass;
private:
    int topSecret;
};

class YourOtherClass
{
public:
    void change( YourClass yc )
};

void YourOtherClass::change( YourClass yc )
{
    yc.topSecret++;    // Can access private data
}
```

The **friend** declaration is not affected by the **public** or **private** keywords; you can place it anywhere in the class's declaration.

Notice that the **friend** declaration appears in `YourClass`. When you write `YourClass`, you specify those classes that you wish to have access to `YourClass`'s private data. Another programmer cannot write a class called `HisClass` and declare it to be a friend in order to gain access. For example:

```
class HisClass
{
// Cannot declare itself to be a friend of YourClass
public:
    void change( YourClass yc )
};

void HisClass::change( YourClass yc )
{
    yc.topSecret++;    // Error: can't access private data
}
```

Thus, you control who has access to the classes you write.

Notice that the **friend** keyword provides access in one direction only. While YourOtherClass is a friend of YourClass, the reverse is not true. Friendship is not mutual unless explicitly specified as such.

A list class demonstrates the usefulness of friend classes more realistically. Suppose you want to maintain a list of names and phone numbers, and you want to be able to specify someone's name and find his or her phone number. You could write a class like the following:

```
#include <string.h>

struct Record
{
    char name[30];
    char number[10];
};
const int MAXLENGTH = 100;

class PhoneList
{
friend class PhoneIter;
public:
    PhoneList();
    int add( const Record &newRec );
    Record *search( char *searchKey );
private:
    Record aray[MAXLENGTH];
    int firstEmpty;          // First unused element
};

PhoneList::PhoneList()
{
    firstEmpty = 0;
}

int PhoneList::add( const Record &newRec )
{
    if( firstEmpty < MAXLENGTH - 1 )
    {
        aray[firstEmpty++] = newRec;
        return 1;   // Indicate success
    }
    else return 0;
}
```

```
Record *PhoneList::search( char *searchKey )
{
    for( int i = 0; i < firstEmpty; i++ )
    if( !strcmp( aray[i].name, searchKey ) )
        return &aray[i];

    return 0;
}
```

Each PhoneList object contains an array of Record structures. You can add new entries and search through the existing entries by specifying a name. You can create as many PhoneList objects as you need for storing separate lists of names.

Now suppose you want to examine each of the entries stored in a PhoneList object, one by one; that is, you want to "iterate" through all the entries. One way to do this is to write an iterator class that is a friend of the PhoneList class.

Here's the friend class PhoneIter:

```
class PhoneIter
{
public:
    PhoneIter( PhoneList &m );
    Record *getFirst();
    Record *getLast();
    Record *getNext();
    Record *getPrev();
private:
    PhoneList *const mine;       // Pointer to a PhoneList object
    int currIndex;
};

PhoneIter::PhoneIter( const PhoneList &m )
    : mine( &m )            // Initialize the constant member
{
    currIndex = 0;
}

Record *PhoneIter::getFirst()
{
    currIndex = 0;
    return &(mine->aray[currIndex]);
}
Record *PhoneIter::getLast()
{
    currIndex = mine->firstEmpty - 1;
    return &(mine->aray[currIndex]);
}
```

```
Record *PhoneIter::getNext()
{
    if( currIndex < mine->firstEmpty - 1 )
    {
        currIndex++;
        return &(mine->aray[currIndex]);
    }
    else return 0;
}

Record *PhoneIter::getPrev()
{
    if( currIndex > 0 )
    {
        currIndex--;
        return &(mine->aray[currIndex]);
    }
    else return 0;
}
```

When you declare a PhoneIter object, you initialize it with a PhoneList object. The PhoneIter object stores your current position within the list. Here's a function that demonstrates the use of a PhoneIter object:

```
void printList( PhoneList aList )
{
    Record *each;
    PhoneIter anIter( aList );

    each = anIter.getFirst();
    cout << each->name << ' ' << each->number << '\n';
    while( each = anIter.getNext() )
    {
        cout << each->name << ' ' << each->number << '\n';
    }
}
```

By calling the getNext and getPrev member functions, you can move the current position forward or back, reading the elements in the list at the same time. With the getFirst and getLast functions, you can start at either end of the list.

The PhoneIter class is useful because you can declare several iterator objects for a particular PhoneList class. Thus, you can maintain several current positions within the list, like bookmarks, and you can move each one back and forth independently. This type of functionality is cumbersome to implement using only member functions.

An important characteristic of the PhoneList class is that users of the class don't know that it's implemented with an array. You could replace the array with a doubly linked list without affecting the class's interface. You would have to rewrite the add function to append a new node to the linked list and rewrite the search function to traverse the list, but the prototypes of those functions would remain the same as they are now. Programs that call the add and search functions don't have to be modified at all.

If you were to rewrite the PhoneList class in this way, you would also have to rewrite the PhoneIter class. Instead of containing the index of the current element, each PhoneIter object would contain a pointer to the current node. However, the available operations would not change; the class's interface would remain the same. (Together, the PhoneList and PhoneIter classes form an "abstract" phone list, which is defined only by its operations, not by its internal workings. Abstraction is discussed in Chapter 9, "Fundamentals of Object-Oriented Design.")

When you use the friend mechanism in C++, you are no longer writing a class that stands alone; you are writing two or more classes that are always used together. If you rewrite one class, you must also rewrite the other(s). You should therefore use the friend mechanism very sparingly; otherwise, you may have to rewrite large amounts of code whenever you change one class.

Friend Functions

You can also declare a single function with the **friend** keyword, instead of an entire class. For example:

```
class YourClass
{
friend void YourFunction( YourClass yc );
private:
    int topSecret;
};

void YourFunction( YourClass yc )
{
    yc.topSecret++;    // Modify private data
}
```

Friend functions are often used for operator overloading. For more information, see Chapter 8, "Operator Overloading and Conversion Functions."

Arrays of Class Objects

You can declare arrays of objects in the same way that you can declare arrays of any other data type. For example:

```
Date birthdays[10];
```

When you declare an array of objects, the constructor is called for each element in the array. If you want to be able to declare arrays without initializing them, the class must have a default constructor (that is, one that can be called without arguments). In the above example, the default `Date` constructor is called, initializing each element in the array to January 1, 1.

You can also provide initializers for each element in the array by explicitly calling the constructor with arguments. If you don't provide enough initializers for the entire array, the default constructor is called for the remaining elements. For example:

```
Date birthdays[10] = { Date( 2, 10, 1950 ),
                       Date( 9, 16, 1960 ),
                       Date( 7, 31, 1953 ),
                       Date( 1, 3, 1970 ),
                       Date( 12, 2, 1963 ) };
```

The previous example calls the `Date` constructor that takes three parameters for the first five elements of the array, and the default constructor for the remaining five elements.

Notice the syntax for calling a constructor explicitly. Unlike the usual syntax, which declares an object and initializes it, this syntax creates an object with a particular value directly. This is analogous to specifying the integer constant 123 instead of declaring an integer variable and initializing it.

If the class has a constructor that takes only one argument, you can specify just the argument as the initializer for an element. You can also mix different styles of initializer. For example:

```
String message[10] = { "First line of message\n",
                       "Second line of message\n",
                       String( "Third line of message\n"),
                       String( '-', 25 ),
                       String() };
```

In the previous example, the single-parameter constructor is called for the first three elements of the array, implicitly for the first two elements and explicitly for the third. The two-parameter constructor is called explicitly for the fourth element. The default constructor is called explicitly for the fifth element and implicitly for the remaining five elements.

The Free Store and Class Arrays

You can also use the **new** operator to dynamically allocate arrays of objects. For example:

```
String *text;
text = new String[5];
```

There is no way to provide initializers for the elements of an array allocated with **new**. The default constructor is called for each element in the array.

When you deallocate an array of objects with the **delete** operator, you must specify a pair of empty brackets to indicate that an array is being deleted. The consequences of using the wrong syntax are serious. For example:

```
delete text;      // Incorrect syntax for deleting array
```

When the previous statement is executed, the compiler treats text as a pointer to a String, so it calls the destructor for the object *text, and then it deallocates the space pointed to by text. However, text points to an entire array, not just a single object. The destructor is called only for text[0], not for text[1] through text[4]. As a result, the character buffers allocated for those four String objects are never deallocated. This is illustrated in Figure 6.2.

If you use the correct syntax for deleting arrays, the destructor is called properly. For example:

```
delete [] text;
```

This syntax tells the compiler that text points to an array. The compiler looks up the size of the array, which was stored when the array was first allocated with **new**. Then the compiler calls the destructor for all the elements in the array, from text[0] to text[4]. The destructor deallocates the buffer for each of the objects in turn, and then the compiler deallocates the space pointed to by text. This is illustrated in Figure 6.3.

In earlier versions of C++, you had to specify the array size within the brackets when you called **delete**, and errors resulted if you specified a different size than used in the **new** call. In the latest version of C++, the compiler stores the sizes of all arrays allocated with **new** and ignores numbers specified when calling **delete**.

Figure 6.2   Incorrect Behavior for Deleting an Array

Steps taken during `delete text;`

before deletion

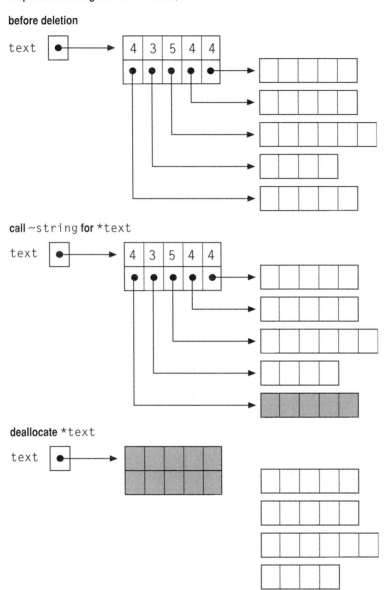

call ~string for *text

deallocate *text

Figure 6.3 Correct Behavior for Deleting an Array

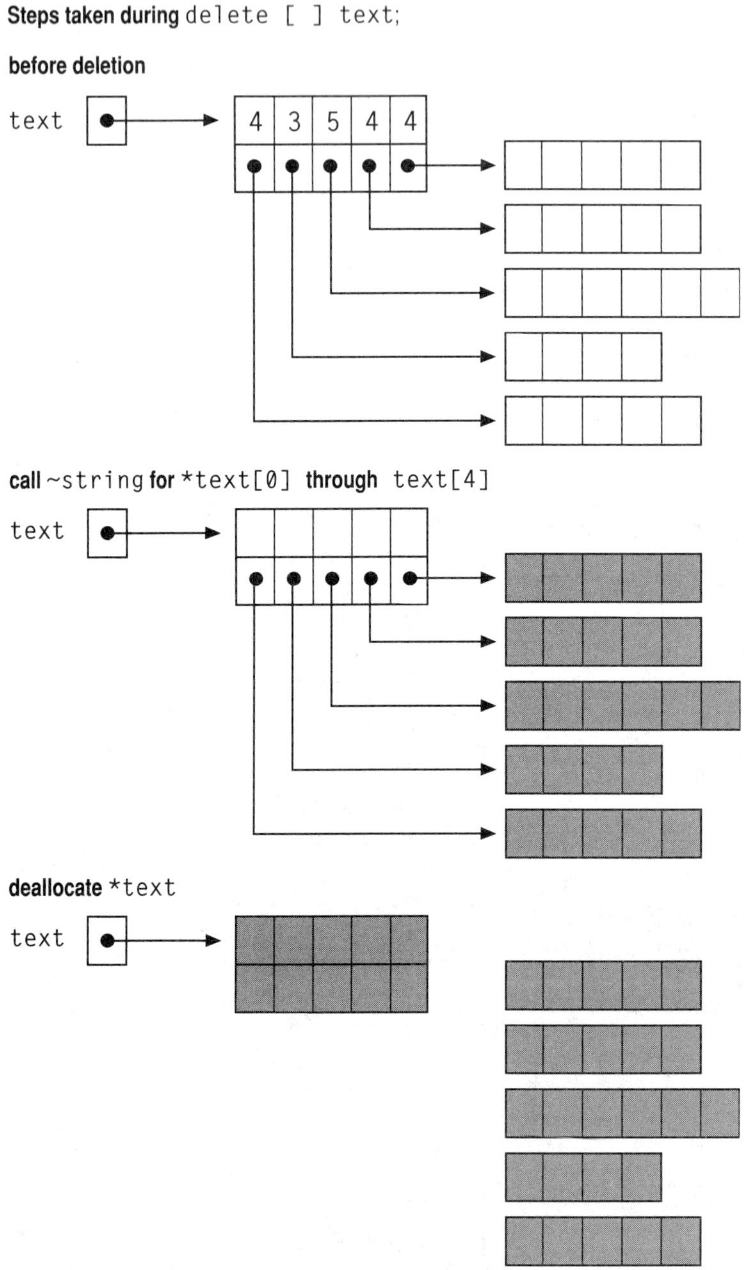
Steps taken during delete [ ] text;
before deletion
text
4 3 5 4 4
call ~string for *text[0] through text[4]
text
deallocate *text
text

If you're using a class that has no destructor, it is possible, although inadvisable, to delete an array of objects without specifying the [ ]. For example, because the `Date` class has no destructor, the following example works:

```
// BAD TECHNIQUE: deleting array of objects without []
//      for a class that has no destructor
Date *appointments;

appointments = new Date[10];
// Use the array
delete appointments;    // Same as delete [] appointments;
```

In this case, the compiler notices that the `Date` class doesn't have a destructor, so it immediately deallocates the space pointed to by `appointments`. Because the `Date` objects have no buffers attached to them, no problems result from the lack of the destructor calls.

However, you should always use the [ ] syntax when deleting arrays, even for classes that have no destructors. The reason is that a class may be reimplemented later on, and the new implementation could perform dynamic memory allocation and require a destructor. (For example, you might implement a class using an array and then switch to a linked list later. The first version doesn't require a destructor, but the second version does.) If your programs assume that the class doesn't have a destructor, they might have to be modified later on. By consistently using the [ ] syntax whenever you delete arrays, you ensure that your programs work properly no matter how the class is implemented.

Advanced Free Store Techniques

C++ gives you much more control over dynamic allocation of memory than C does. The following sections describe ways you can customize the memory allocation in your program.

The _set_new_handler Function

The C function **malloc** returns **NULL** when it cannot allocate the requested amount of memory. When programming in C, it is good practice to check for a **NULL** return value every time you call **malloc**. This way, your program can exit gracefully instead of crashing as a result of trying to dereference a **NULL** pointer.

Similarly, the **new** operator returns 0 when it cannot allocate the requested amount of memory. Just as in C, you can check for a 0 return value every time you call **new**. However, C++ provides a more convenient alternative in the **_set_new_handler** function (declared in the include file NEW.H).

The **_set_new_handler** function takes a function pointer as an argument. This pointer must point to an error-handling function that you write. By calling **_set_new_handler**, you install this function as the error handler for the free store. When **new** cannot allocate the memory requested, it checks to see if an error handler has been installed. If no error handler is installed (which is the default), **new** returns 0. If you have installed an error handler, **new** calls it.

You can write a simple error-handling function that prints an error message and exits the program. For example:

```
// HANDLER.CPP
// Free store exhaustion and the _set_new_handler function
#include <iostream.h>
#include <stdlib.h>
#include <new.h>

int all_gone( size_t size )
{
    cerr << "\n\aThe free store is empty\n";
    exit( 1 );
    return 0;
}

void main()
{
    _set_new_handler( all_gone );
    long total = 0;
    while( 1 )
    {
        char *gobble = new char[1000000];
        total += 1000000;
        cout << "Got 1000000 for a total of " << total << endl;
    }
}
```

This example executes a loop that consumes memory and displays the total amount of memory currently allocated. When **new** cannot allocate any more memory, it calls the all_gone function, which prints an error message and exits. Note that the all_gone function takes a parameter of type **size_t**, which represents the size of the block requested when **new** failed, and that it returns an integer. Any error-handling function you write must have this parameter and return type.

The previous example might print the following messages, depending on how much memory is available:

```
Got 1000000 for a total of 1000000
Got 1000000 for a total of 2000000
Got 1000000 for a total of 3000000
Got 1000000 for a total of 4000000
Got 1000000 for a total of 5000000
The free store is empty
```

An error-handling function like this removes the need for you to check the return value of **new** every time you call it. You can write code to handle the possibility of memory exhaustion in just one place, rather than throughout your program.

Overloading the new and delete Operators

C++ lets you redefine the behavior of the **new** and **delete** operators if you want to perform customized memory management. For example, suppose you want **new** to initialize the contents of a memory block to zero before returning the allocated memory. You can implement this by writing special functions named **operator new** and **operator delete**. For example:

```
// NEWDEL.CPP
// Customized new and delete
#include <iostream.h>
#include <stdlib.h>
#include <stddef.h>

// ------------ Overloaded new operator
void *operator new( size_t size )
{
    void *rtn = calloc( 1, size );
    return rtn;
}

// ---------- Overloaded delete operator
void operator delete( void *ptr )
{
    free( ptr );
}
```

```
void main()
{
    // Allocate a zero-filled array
    int *ip = new int[10];
    // Display the array
    for( int i = 0; i < 10; i++ )
        cout << " " << ip[i];
    cout << endl;
    // Release the memory
    delete [] ip;
}
```

Note that the **new** operator takes a parameter of type **size_t**. This parameter holds the size of the object being allocated, and the compiler automatically sets its value whenever you use **new**. Also note that the **new** operator returns a **void** pointer. Any **new** operator you write must have this parameter and return type.

In this particular example, **new** calls the standard C function **calloc** to allocate memory and initialize it to zero.

The **delete** operator takes a **void** pointer as a parameter. This parameter points to the block to be deallocated. Also note that the **delete** operator has a **void** return type. Any **delete** operator you write must have this parameter and return type.

In this example, **delete** simply calls the standard C function **free** to deallocate the memory.

Note When compiling the NEWDEL.CPP and NEWDEL2.CPP example programs in Visual C++ Standard Edition 4.0, you must specify a Release Build instead of a Debug Build. This is because a debug version of **delete** is already provided with Visual C++ Standard Edition 4.0 as part of the run-time library, and you cannot define two versions of the **delete** operator.

Redefining **new** to initialize memory this way does not eliminate the call to a class's constructor when you dynamically allocate an object. Thus, if you allocate a Date object using your version of **new**, the Date constructor is still called to initialize the object after the **new** operator returns the block of memory.

You can also redefine **new** to take additional parameters. The following example defines a **new** operator that fills memory with the character specified when you allocate memory:

```
// NEWDEL2.CPP
// new and delete with character fill
#include <iostream.h>
#include <stdlib.h>
#include <string.h>
#include <stddef.h>
```

```
// ------------- Overloaded new operator
void *operator new( size_t size, int filler )
{
    void *rtn;
    if( (rtn = malloc( size )) != NULL )
        memset( rtn, filler, size );
    return rtn;
}

// ----------- Overloaded delete operator
void operator delete( void *ptr )
{
    free( ptr );
}

void main()
{
    // Allocate an asterisk-filled array
    char *cp = new( '*' ) char[10];
    // Display the array
    for( int i = 0; i < 10; i++ )
        cout << " " << cp[i];
    cout << endl;
    // Release the memory
    delete [] cp;
}
```

Notice that when you call this version of **new**, you specify the additional argument in parentheses.

Class-Specific new and delete Operators

You can also write versions of the **new** and **delete** operators that are specific to a particular class. This lets you perform memory management that is customized for a class's individual characteristics.

For example, you might know that there will never be more than a certain small number of instances of a class at any one time, but they'll be allocated and deallocated frequently. You can use this information to write class-specific versions of **new** and **delete** that work faster than the global versions. You can declare an array large enough to hold all the instances of the class and then have **new** and **delete** manage the array.

To write class-specific **new** and **delete** operators, you declare member functions named **operator new** and **operator delete**. These operators take precedence over the global **new** and **delete** operators, in the same way that any member function takes precedence over a global function with the same name. These operators are called whenever you dynamically allocate objects of that class. For example:

```
// NEWDEL3.CPP
// Class-specific new and delete operators
#include <iostream.h>
#include <string.h>
#include <stddef.h>

const int MAXNAMES = 10;

class Name
{
public:
    Name( const char *s ) { strncpy( name, s, 25 ); }
    void display() const { cout << name << endl; }
    void *operator new( size_t size );
    void operator delete( void *ptr );
    ~Name() {};    // do-nothing destructor
private:
    char name[25];
};
// -------- Simple memory pool to handle fixed number of Names
char pool[MAXNAMES] [sizeof( Name )];
int inuse[MAXNAMES];

// -------- Overloaded new operator for the Name class
void *Name::operator new( size_t size )
{
    for( int p = 0; p < MAXNAMES; p++ )
    if( !inuse[p] )
    {
        inuse[p] = 1;
        return pool + p;
    }
    return 0;
}
```

```
// --------- Overloaded delete operator for the Names class
void Name::operator delete( void *ptr )
{
    inuse[((char *)ptr - pool[0]) / sizeof( Name )] = 0;
}

void main()
{
    Name *directory[MAXNAMES];
    char name[25];

    for( int i = 0; i < MAXNAMES; i++ )
    {
        cout << "\nEnter name # " << i+1 << ": ";
        cin >> name;
        directory[i] = new Name( name );
    }
    for( i = 0; i < MAXNAMES; i++ )
    {
        directory[i]->display();
        delete directory[i];
    }
}
```

This program declares a global array called pool that can store all the Name objects expected. There is also an associated integer array called inuse, which contains true/false flags that indicate whether the corresponding entry in the pool is in use.

When the statement directory[i] = new Name(name) is executed, the compiler calls the class's **new** operator. The **new** operator finds an unused entry in pool, marks it as used, and returns its address. Then the compiler calls Name's constructor, which uses that memory and initializes it with a character string. Finally, a pointer to the resulting object is assigned to an entry in directory.

When the statement delete directory[i] is executed, the compiler calls Name's destructor. In this example, the destructor does nothing; it is defined only as a placeholder. Then the compiler calls the class's **delete** operator. The **delete** operator finds the specified object's location in the array and marks it as unused, so the space is available for subsequent allocations.

Note that **new** is called before the constructor, and that **delete** is called after the destructor. The following example illustrates this more clearly by printing messages when each function is called:

```cpp
// NEWDEL4.CPP
// Class-specific new and delete operators with constructor, destructor
#include <iostream.h>
#include <malloc.h>

class Name
{
public:
    Name()  { cout << "\nName's constructor running"; }
    void *operator new( size_t size );
    void operator delete( void *ptr );
    ~Name() { cout << "\nName's destructor running"; }
private:
    char name[25];
};

// -------- Simple memory pool to handle one Name
char pool[sizeof( Name )];

// -------- Overloaded new operator for the Name class
void *Name::operator new( size_t )
{
    cout << "\nName's new running";
    return pool;
}

// --------- Overloaded delete operator for the Name class
void Name::operator delete( void *p )
{
    cout << "\nName's delete running";
}

void main()
{
    cout << "\nExecuting: nm = new Name";
    Name *nm = new Name;
    cout << "\nExecuting: delete nm";
    delete nm;
}
```

The previous example does nothing with the class except display the following messages as the various functions execute:

```
Executing: nm = new Name
Name's new running
Name's constructor running
Executing: delete nm
Name's destructor running
Name's delete running
```

One consequence of the order in which **new** and **delete** are called is that they are static member functions, even if they are not declared with the **static** keyword. This is because the **new** operator is called before the class's constructor is called; the object does not exist yet, so it would be meaningless for **new** to access any of its members. Similarly, the **delete** operator is called after the destructor is called and the object no longer exists. To prevent **new** and **delete** from accessing any nonstatic members, the operators are always considered static member functions.

The class-specific **new** and **delete** operators are not called when you allocate or deallocate an array of objects; instead the global **new** and **delete** are called for array allocations. You can explicitly call the global versions of the operators when you allocate a single object by using the scope resolution operator (**::**). For example:

```
Name *nm = ::new Name;    // Use global new
```

If you have also redefined the global **new** operator, this syntax calls your version of the operator. The same syntax works for **delete**.

Inheritance and Polymorphism

Besides making it easy for you to define new data types, C++ also lets you express relationships between those types. This is done with two of C++'s features: The first is "inheritance," which lets you define one type to be a subcategory of another. The second is "polymorphism," which lets you use related types together.

This chapter describes the mechanics of inheritance and polymorphism. In Part 3, "Object-Oriented Design," you'll see how these features play a role when you design a program.

This chapter covers the following topics:

- Base and derived classes

- Redefining members of a base class

- Conversions between base and derived classes

- Virtual functions and late binding

- Abstract classes

- The **protected** keyword

Before describing in detail C++'s features for handling related types, let's consider how you might handle them in C.

Handling Related Types in C

Suppose you need a program that maintains a database of all the employees in a company. The company has several different types of employee: regular employees, salespersons, managers, temporary employees, and so on, and your program must be able to handle all of them.

If you're writing this program in C, you could define a structure type called employee that has fields for the name, birth date, social security number, and other characteristics. However, each type of employee requires slightly different information. For example, a regular employee's salary is based on an hourly wage and the number of hours worked, while a salesperson's salary also includes a commission on the number of sales made, and a manager's salary is a fixed amount per week.

It's difficult to find a way to represent the information about each employee. You could define a different structure type for each type of employee, but then you couldn't write a function that worked on all kinds of employees; you couldn't pass a manager structure to a function expecting an employee structure. Another possibility is to include all the possible fields in the employee structure type, but that would be a waste of space, because several fields would be empty for any given employee.

One solution in C is to define a structure that contains a union. For example:

```c
/* Example of implementing related types in C */

struct wage_pay
{
    double wage;
    double hrs;
};

struct sales_pay
{
    double wage;
    double hrs;
    double commission;
    double sales_made;
};

struct mgr_pay
{
    double weekly_salary;
};

enum { WAGE_EMPLOYEE, SALESPERSON, MANAGER } EMPLOYEE_TYPE;
```

```
struct employee
{
    char name[30];
    EMPLOYEE_TYPE type;
    union
    {
        struct wage_pay worker;
        struct sales_pay seller;
        struct mgr_pay mgr;
    };                              // Anonymous union
};
```

The employee structure contains a union of the various salary structures. The program uses the type field to indicate the type of employee and to keep track of which form of salary is stored in the union.

Now consider how you would compute the salary of an employee. You might write a function that looks like this:

```
/* Example of type-specific processing in C */

double compute_pay( struct employee *emp )
{
    switch( emp->type )
    {
    case WAGE_EMPLOYEE:
        return emp->worker.hrs * emp->worker.wage;
        break;
    case SALESPERSON:
        return emp->seller.hrs * emp->seller.wage +
                emp->seller.commissions * emp->seller.sales_made;
        break;
    case MANAGER:
        return emp->mgr.weekly_salary;
        break;
    // ...
    };
}
```

This function uses the value of the type field to determine how it accesses the contents of the union. This way, the function can perform a different salary computation for each type of employee.

Salary computation is only one example of a task that is different for each type of employee. The employee-database program might use unions and **switch** statements for a wide variety of tasks, such as health plan management or vacation computation.

These **switch** statements have a couple of disadvantages:

- They can be difficult to read, especially if there is common processing for two or more types. It's also difficult to isolate the code that describes a particular type; for example, the code to handle the SalesPerson class is spread throughout the program.

- They are difficult to maintain. If you add a new type of employee, you have to add a new **case** statement that handles that type to every **switch** statement in the program. This makes updating the program error-prone, because it's possible to overlook a **switch** statement somewhere. In addition, every time you modify the code that handles one type, you must recompile the code that handles all the other types. This can be time-consuming when you're testing code for a new type of employee.

There are other ways to write this program in C, but they require much more programming effort. C doesn't provide an easy and maintainable way to express relations among multiple user-defined types. One of the goals in designing C++ was to remedy C's weakness in this area.

Handling Related Types in C++

Suppose you're writing the employee-database program in C++. First, define a class called Employee that describes the common characteristics of all employees. For example:

```
class Employee
{
public:
    Employee();
    Employee( const char *nm );
    const char *getName() const;
private:
    char name[30];
};
```

For simplicity, this employee class stores only a name, though it could store many other characteristics as well, such as a birth date, a social security number, and an address.

Next, you can define a WageEmployee class that describes a particular type of employee: those who are paid by the hour. These employees have the characteristics common to all employees, plus some additional ones.

There are two ways you can use Employee when you define the WageEmployee class. One way is to give WageEmployee an Employee object as a data member. However, that doesn't properly describe the relationship between the two types. A wage-earning employee doesn't contain a generic employee; rather, a wage-earning employee is a special type of employee.

The second possibility is inheritance, which makes one class a special type of another. You can make WageEmployee inherit from Employee with the following syntax:

```
class WageEmployee : public Employee
{
public:
    WageEmployee( const char *nm );
    void setWage( double wg );
    void setHours( double hrs );
private:
    double wage;
    double hours;
};
```

WageEmployee is a "derived class," and Employee is its "base class." To declare a derived class, you follow its name with a colon and the keyword **public**, followed by the name of its base class (you can also use the keyword **private**; this is described in the section "Public and Private Base Classes"). In the declaration of the derived class, you declare the members that are specific to it; that is, you describe the additional qualities that distinguish it from the base class.

Each instance of WageEmployee contains all of Employee's data members, in addition to its own. You can call any of Employee's or WageEmployee's member functions for a WageEmployee object. For example:

```
WageEmployee aWorker( "Bill Shapiro" );
const char *str;

aWorker.setHours( 40.0 );    // call WageEmployee::setHours
str = aWorker.getName();     // call Employee::getname
```

Figure 7.1 illustrates the members contained in Employee and WageEmployee.

Figure 7.1 Data Members in Base and Derived Classes

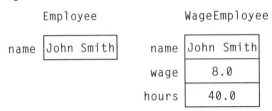

The member functions of a derived class do not have access to the private members of its base class. Therefore, the member functions of `WageEmployee` cannot access the private members of its base class `Employee`. For example, suppose you write the following function:

```
void WageEmployee::printName() const
{
    cout << "Worker's name: "
        << name << endl;        // Error: name is private
                                //       member of Employee
}
```

Because `name` is one of the private members of the base class, it is inaccessible to any member function of `WageEmployee`.

This restriction may seem surprising. After all, if a `WageEmployee` is a kind of `Employee`, why shouldn't it have access to its own `Employee` characteristics? This restriction is designed to enforce encapsulation. If a derived class had access to its base class's private data, then anyone could access the private data of a class by simply deriving a new class from it. The point of making data private is to prevent programmers who use your class from writing code that depends on its implementation details, and this includes programmers who write derived classes. If the original class's implementation were changed, every class that derived from it would have to be rewritten as well.

Consequently, a derived class must use the base class's public interface, just as any other user of the class must. You could rewrite the previous example as follows:

```
void WageEmployee::printName() const
{
    cout << "Worker's name: "
        << getName() << endl; // Call Employee::getName
}
```

This function uses `Employee`'s public interface to get the information it needs.

To make this C++ example more like the employee example in C, you can also define classes that describe salespersons and managers. Because salespersons are a kind of wage-earning employee, you can derive the `SalesPerson` class from the `WageEmployee` class.

```
class SalesPerson : public WageEmployee
{
public:
    SalesPerson( const char *nm );
    void setCommission( double comm );
    void setSales( double sales );
private:
    double commission;
    double salesMade;
};
```

A `SalesPerson` object contains all the data members defined by `Employee` and `WageEmployee`, as well as the ones defined by `SalesPerson`. Similarly, you can call any of the member functions defined in these three classes for a `SalesPerson` object. (The `Employee` class is considered an "indirect" base class of `SalesPerson`, while the `WageEmployee` class is a "direct" base class of `SalesPerson`.)

Notice that this declaration means that `WageEmployee` is both a derived class and a base class. It derives from the `Employee` class and serves as the base for the `SalesPerson` class. You can define as many levels of inheritance as you want.

Managers are a type of employee that receives a fixed salary. Accordingly, you can derive the `Manager` class from `Employee`, as follows:

```
class Manager : public Employee
{
public:
    Manager( const char *nm );
    void setSalary( double salary );
private:
    double weeklySalary;
};
```

The inheritance relationships among all of these classes are shown in Figure 7.2. This figure illustrates a "class hierarchy," or a group of user-defined types organized according to their relationship to one another. The class at the top represents the most general type, and the classes at the bottom represent the more specialized types. As you'll learn in Part 3, "Object-Oriented Design," designing an appropriate class hierarchy is one of the most important steps in writing an object-oriented program.

Figure 7.2 Employee Class Hierarchy

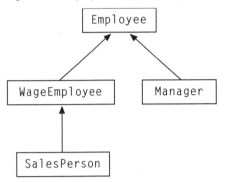

Notice that Employee acts as a base class for more than one class (WageEmployee and Manager). Any number of derived classes can inherit from a given base class.

Also notice that the Manager class shares members only with Employee. It doesn't have any of the members defined by WageEmployee or SalesPerson.

Redefining Members of the Base Class

Now consider how to compute the weekly pay of the various types of employees. You can define a member function for WageEmployee called computePay. For example:

```
double WageEmployee::computePay() const
{
    return wage * hours;
}
```

You can also give the SalesPerson class a computePay member function, just as with its base class. As mentioned in the last two paragraphs of "Handling Related Types in C++," this function cannot access any private members of WageEmployee, so the following function generates an error:

```
double SalesPerson::computePay() const
{
    return hours * wage +            // Error: hours and
           commission * salesMade;   //    wages are private
}
```

You must call a public member function of the base class. The following implementation calls such a function, but it does not work either:

```
double SalesPerson::computePay() const
{
    return computePay() +             // Bad recursive call
           commission * salesMade;
}
```

The compiler assumes that computePay refers to SalesPerson's version of the function. This results in infinite recursion. You must use the scope resolution operator (::) to specify the base class's version of the function. For example:

```
double SalesPerson::computePay() const
{
    // Call base class's version of computePay
    return WageEmployee::computePay() +
           commission * salesMade;
}
```

This technique is commonly used when redefining a member function in a derived class. The derived class's version calls the base class's version and then performs any additional operations needed.

When you call a redefined member function for an object of a derived class, the derived class's version of the function is used. For example, when using a SalesPerson object, any call to computePay invokes SalesPerson's version of the function. For example:

```
SalesPerson aSeller( "John Smith" );

aSeller.setHours( 40.0 );
aSeller.setWage( 6.0 );
aSeller.setCommission( 0.05 );
aSeller.setSales( 2000.0 );
//   Call SalesPerson::computePay
cout << "Seller salary: "
     << aSeller.computePay() << endl;
```

Within this class, the `computePay` function defaults to the definition in the `SalesPerson` class. Again, to call the base class's version of the function, you must use the scope resolution operator. For example:

```
cout << "Seller base salary: "
    << aSeller.WageEmployee::computePay() << endl;
```

You can also give the `Manager` class a `computePay` member function:

```
double Manager::computePay() const
{
    return weeklySalary;
}
```

This function involves no redefining of the similarly named functions in `WageEmployee` or `SalesPerson`, because neither of those classes are derived or base classes of `Manager`.

Derived Class Constructors

An instance of a derived class contains all the members of the base class, and all of those members must be initialized during construction. Consequently, the base class's constructor has to be called by the derived class's constructor. When you write the constructor for a derived class, you must specify a "base initializer," using syntax similar to that of the member initializer list for constructing member objects. Place a colon after the argument list of the derived class's constructor, and follow it with the name of the base class and an argument list. For example:

```
// Constructor function for WageEmployee
WageEmployee::WageEmployee( const char *nm )
    : Employee( nm )
{
    wage = 0.0;
    hours = 0.0;
}

// Constructor function for SalesPerson
SalesPerson::SalesPerson( const char *nm )
    : WageEmployee( nm )
{
    commission = 0.0;
    salesMade = 0.0;
}
```

```
// Constructor function for Manager
Manager::Manager( const char *nm )
    : Employee( nm )
{
    weeklySalary = 0.0;
}
```

When you declare an object of a derived class, the compiler executes the constructor for the base class first and then executes the constructor for the derived class. (If the derived class contains member objects, their constructors are executed after the base class's constructor, but before the derived class's constructor.)

You can omit the base initializer if the base class has a default constructor. As with member objects, however, you should use the base initializer syntax rather than perform redundant initialization.

If you're defining a derived class that also has member objects, you can specify both a member initializer list and a base initializer. However, you cannot define member initializers for member objects defined in the base class, because that would permit multiple initializations.

Conversions Between Base and Derived Classes

Because a salesperson is a kind of wage-earning employee, it makes sense to be able to use a SalesPerson object whenever a WageEmployee object is needed. To support this relationship, C++ lets you implicitly convert an instance of a derived class into an instance of a base class. For example:

```
WageEmployee aWorker;
SalesPerson aSeller( "John Smith" );

aWorker = aSeller;    // Convert SalesPerson to WageEmployee
                      //    derived => base
```

All the members of the SalesPerson object receive the values of the corresponding members in the WageEmployee object. However, the reverse assignment is not legal:

```
aSeller = aWorker;    // Error; cannot convert
```

Because SalesPerson has members that WageEmployee doesn't, their values would be undefined after such an assignment. This restriction follows the conceptual relationship between the types of employee: A worker is not necessarily a salesperson.

You can also implicitly convert a pointer to a derived class object into a pointer to a base class object. For example:

```
Employee *empPtr;
WageEmployee aWorker( "Bill Shapiro" );
SalesPerson aSeller( "John Smith" );
Manager aBoss( "Mary Brown" );

empPtr = &aWorker;     // Convert WageEmployee * to Employee *
empPtr = &aSeller;     // Convert SalesPerson * to Employee *
empPtr = &aBoss;       // Convert Manager * to Employee *
```

You can use a pointer to an `Employee` to point to a `WageEmployee` object, a `SalesPerson` object, or a `Manager` object.

When you refer to an object through a pointer, the type of the pointer determines which member functions you can call. If you refer to a derived class object with a base class pointer, you can call only the functions defined by the base class. For example:

```
SalesPerson aSeller( "John Smith" );
SalesPerson *salePtr;
WageEmployee *wagePtr;

salePtr = &aSeller;
wagePtr = &aSeller;

wagePtr->setHours( 40.0 );       // Call WageEmployee::setHours
salePtr->setWage( 6.0 );         // Call WageEmployee::setWage
wagePtr->setSales( 1000.0 );     // Error;
                                 //    no WageEmployee::setSales
salePtr->setSales( 1000.0 );     // Call SalesPerson::setSales
salePtr->setCommission( 0.05 );  // Call SalesPerson::setCommission
```

Both `wagePtr` and `salePtr` point to a single `SalesPerson` object. You cannot call `setSales` through `wagePtr`, because `WageEmployee` doesn't define that member function. You have to use `salePtr` to call the member functions that `SalesPerson` defines.

If you call a member function that is defined by both the base class and the derived class, the function that is called depends on the type of the pointer. For example:

```
double base, total;

base = wagePtr->computePay();    // Call WageEmployee::computePay
total = salePtr->computePay();   // Call SalesPerson::computePay
```

When you use `wagePtr`, you call the version defined by `WageEmployee`. When you use `salePtr`, you call the version defined by `SalesPerson`.

To perform the reverse conversion (that is, from a pointer to a base class to a pointer to a derived class), you must use an explicit cast:

```
WageEmployee *wagePtr = &aSeller;
SalesPerson *salePtr;

salePtr = (SalesPerson *)wagePtr;   // Explicit cast required
                                    //     base => derived
```

This conversion is dangerous, because you can't be sure what type of object the base class pointer points to. Suppose `empPtr` points to something other than a `SalesPerson` object:

```
Employee *empPtr = &aWorker;
SalesPerson *salePtr;

salePtr = (SalesPerson *)empPtr;   // Legal, but incorrect
salePtr->setCommission( 0.05 );    // Error: aWorker has no
                                   //     setCommission member
```

This can cause your program to crash. Accordingly, you should be extremely careful when converting a base class pointer to a derived class pointer.

Collections Using Base Class Pointers

The conversion from a derived class pointer to a base class pointer is very useful. For example, if you have a function that expects a pointer to an `Employee` as a parameter, you can pass this function a pointer to any type of employee.

One application of this is to maintain a collection of employees. You could write an `EmployeeList` class that maintains a linked list, each node holding a pointer to an `Employee` object. For example:

```
class EmployeeList
{
public:
    EmployeeList();
    add( Employee *newEmp );
    // ...
private:
    // ...
};
```

Using the add function, you can insert any type of employee into an EmployeeList object:

```
EmployeeList myDept;
WageEmployee *wagePtr;
SalesPerson *salePtr;
Manager *mgrPtr;

// Allocate new objects
wagePtr = new WageEmployee( "Bill Shapiro" );
salePtr = new SalesPerson( "John Smith" );
mgrPtr = new Manager( "Mary Brown" );
// Add them to the list
myDept.add( wagePtr );
myDept.add( salePtr );
myDept.add( mgrPtr );
```

Once you have a list of employees, you can manipulate its contents using the Employee class's interface, even though the list contains all different types of employees. For example, you can define an iterator class called EmpIter (like the one described in Chapter 6, "More Features of Classes"), which can return each element of an EmployeeList. Then you can print a list of all the employees' names as follows:

```
void printNames( EmployeeList &dept )
{
    int count = 0;
    Employee *person;
    EmpIter anIter( dept );    // Iterator object
    person = anIter.getNext();
    count++;
    cout << count << ' ' << person->getName() << endl;

    while( person = anIter.getNext() )
    {
        count++;
        cout << count << ' '
             << person->getName() << endl;
    }
}
```

This function iterates through all the elements in the `EmployeeList` object passed as a parameter. For each employee in the list, no matter what type it is, the iterator returns an `Employee` pointer. Using this pointer, the function prints out the employee's name.

The problem with this technique is that you cannot treat an object as anything more than a generic `Employee`. For instance, how could you compute the weekly salary of each employee in the list? If you were to give the `Employee` class a `computePay` function, calling that function wouldn't invoke the `computePay` functions defined in the derived classes. As mentioned earlier, the function that is called is determined by the type of the pointer. Accordingly, calling `computePay` using only `Employee` pointers would perform the same computation for every type of employee, which is clearly unsatisfactory.

What you need is a way to call each class's individual version of `computePay` while still using generic `Employee` pointers. C++ provides a way to do this using virtual functions.

Virtual Functions

A "virtual function" is a member function that you expect to be redefined in derived classes. When you call a virtual function through a pointer to a base class, the derived class's version of the function is executed. This is precisely the opposite behavior of ordinary member functions.

A virtual function is declared by placing the keyword **virtual** before the declaration of the member function in the base class. Global functions and static members cannot be virtual functions. The **virtual** keyword is not necessary in the declarations in the derived classes; all subsequent versions of a virtual function are implicitly declared **virtual**. For example, here is a revised version of the employee class hierarchy that has a virtual `computePay` function:

```
class Employee
{
public:
    Employee( const char *nm );
    const char *getName() const;
    virtual double computePay() const;
    virtual ~Employee() {}
private:
    char name[30];
};

class WageEmployee : public Employee
{
public:
    WageEmployee( const char *nm );
    void setWage( double wg );
    void setHours( double hrs );
    double computePay() const;      // Implicitly virtual
private:
    double wage;
    double hours;
};

class SalesPerson : public WageEmployee
{
public:
    SalesPerson( const char *nm);
    void setCommission( double comm );
    void setSales( double sales );
    double computePay() const;      // Implicitly virtual
private:
    double commission;
    double salesMade;
};

class Manager : public Employee
{
public:
    Manager( const char *nm );
    void setSalary( double salary );
    double computePay() const;      // Implicitly virtual
private:
    double weeklySalary;
};
```

The definitions of each class's version of computePay do not have to be modified. However, because computePay has been added to the base class, a definition for that version of the function is needed:

```
double Employee::computePay() const
{
    cout << "No salary computation defined\n";
    return 0.0;
}
```

This function is needed primarily as a placeholder. It would be called if a plain Employee object were used, or if one of the derived classes did not provide its own definition of computePay.

Now consider what happens when computePay is called through an Employee pointer:

```
Employee *empPtr;
double salary;

empPtr = &aWorker;
salary = empPtr->computePay();   // Call WageEmployee::computePay
empPtr = &aSeller;
salary = empPtr->computePay();   // Call SalesPerson::computePay
empPtr = &aBoss;
salary = empPtr->computePay();   // Call Manager::computePay
```

If computePay hadn't been declared **virtual**, each statement would call Employee::computePay, which would return 0.0. However, because computePay is a virtual function, the function executed is different for each call, even though the calls are exactly the same. The function called is the one appropriate for the actual object that empPtr points to. (You can also use the scope resolution operator to explicitly specify a different version of the function if you want.)

To calculate the weekly payroll for a department, you can write a function like the following:

```
double computePayroll( EmployeeList &dept )
{
    double payroll = 0;
    Employee *person;
    EmpIter anIter( dept );

    person = anIter.getFirst();
    payroll += person->computePay();
    while( person = anIter.getNext() )
    {
        // Call appropriate function
        //     for each type of employee
        payroll += person->computePay();
    }

    return payroll;
}
```

The statement `person->computePay` executes the appropriate function, no matter what type of employee `person` points to.

Polymorphism

The ability to call member functions for an object without specifying the object's exact type is known as "polymorphism." The word "polymorphism" means "the ability to assume many forms," referring to the ability to have a single statement invoke many different functions. In the above example, the pointer `person` can point to any type of employee and the name `computePay` can refer to any of the salary computation functions.

Compare this with the implementation in C provided earlier in this chapter. In C, if all you have is a pointer to an employee, you have to call the `compute_pay` function shown earlier, which must execute a **switch** statement to find the exact type of employee. In C++, the statement `person->computePay()` calls the appropriate function automatically, without requiring you to examine the type of object that `person` points to. (There is only a tiny amount of overhead, as described in the section "How Virtual Functions are Implemented.") No **switch** statement is needed.

Computing salaries is just one example of a task that differs depending on the type of employee. A more realistic `Employee` class would have several virtual functions, one for each type-dependent operation. An employee-database program would have many functions like `computePayroll`, all of which manipulate employees using `Employee` pointers and virtual functions.

In such a program, all the information about any particular type of employee is localized in a single class. You don't have to look at every employee-database function to see how salespersons are handled. All the specialized salesperson processing is contained in the `SalesPerson` class. It's also easy to add a new type of employee, due to a property known as "dynamic binding."

Dynamic Binding

At compile time, the compiler cannot identify the function that is called by the statement `person->computePay()`, because it could be any of several different functions. The compiler must evaluate the statement at run time, when it can tell what type of object `person` points to. This is known as "late binding" or "dynamic binding." This behavior is very different from function calls in C, or nonvirtual function calls in C++. In both these cases, the function call statement is translated at compile time into a call to a fixed function address. This is known as "early binding" or "static binding."

Dynamic binding makes it possible for you to modify the behavior of code that has already been compiled. You can make an existing module handle new types without having to modify the source and recompile it.

For example, suppose that the function `computePayroll` and all the other employee-database functions have been compiled into a module called EMPUTIL.OBJ. Now suppose that you want to define a new type of employee called a `Consultant` and use it with all the existing employee-database functions.

You don't have to modify the source code for `computePayroll` or any other functions in EMPUTIL.OBJ. You simply derive `Consultant` from the `Employee` class, define its member functions in a new source file CONSULT.CPP, and compile it into CONSULT.OBJ. Then you modify your program's user interface to allow users to enter information on consultants. After you've recompiled that portion of the program, you can link it with CONSULT.OBJ and EMPUTIL.OBJ to produce a new executable file.

You can then add `Consultant` objects to the `EmployeeList` object that the program already maintains. When you compute the payroll, the `computePayroll` function works just as it did before. If there are any `Consultant` objects in the list, the statement `person->computePay()` automatically calls `Consultant::computePay`, even though that function didn't exist when the statement was first compiled.

Dynamic binding makes it possible for you to provide a library of classes that other programmers can extend even if they don't have your source code. All you need to distribute are the header files (the .H files) and the compiled object code (.OBJ or .LIB files) for the hierarchy of classes you've written and for the functions that use those classes. Other programmers can derive new classes from yours and redefine the virtual functions you declared. Then the functions that use your classes can handle the classes they've defined.

How Virtual Functions Are Implemented

An obvious question about dynamic binding is "how much overhead is involved?" Is the added convenience gained at the expense of execution speed? Fortunately, virtual functions are very efficient, so calling one takes only slightly longer than calling a normal function.

In some situations, a virtual function call can be implemented as a normal function call—that is, using static binding. For example:

```
SalesPerson aSeller( "John Smith" );
SalesPerson *salePtr;
double salary;

salePtr = &aSeller;
salary = aSeller.computePay();    // Static binding possible
salary = salePtr->computePay();   // Static binding possible
```

In this example, `SalesPerson::computePay` can be called directly because the type of `aSeller` is known. Similarly, the type of the object that `salePtr` points to is known, and again the function can be called directly. In situations where the compiler cannot use static binding, such as the statement `person->computePay()` in the earlier example, the compiler uses dynamic binding.

Dynamic binding is implemented in C++ through the use of a virtual function table, or a "v-table." This is an array of function pointers that the compiler constructs for every class that uses virtual functions. For example, `WageEmployee`, `SalesPerson`, and `Manager` each have their own v-table.

The v-table contains one function pointer for each virtual function in the class. All of the employee classes have only one virtual function, so all of their v-tables contain just one pointer. Each pointer points to the version of the function that is appropriate to that class. Thus, the v-table for `SalesPerson` has a pointer to `SalesPerson::computePay`, and the v-table for `Manager` has a pointer to `Manager::computePay`. This is illustrated in Figure 7.3.

Figure 7.3 How Virtual Functions are Implemented

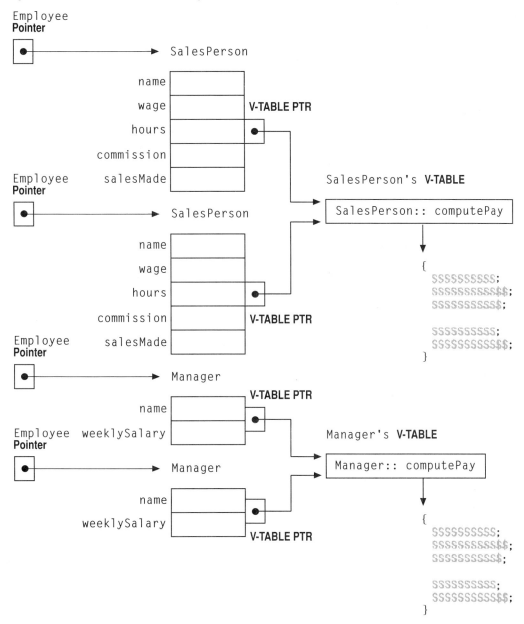

Note that it is not required for a derived class to redefine a virtual function declared in its base class. For example, suppose SalesPerson did not define a computePay function. Then SalesPerson's v-table would contain a pointer to WageEmployee::computePay. If WageEmployee in turn did not define computePay, both classes' v-tables would have pointers to Employee::computePay.

Each instance of a class contains a hidden pointer to the class's v-table. When a statement like person->computePay() is executed, the compiler dereferences the v-table pointer in the object pointed to by person. The compiler then calls the computePay function pointed to by the pointer in the v-table. In this way, the compiler calls a different function for each type of object.

The only difference between a normal function call and a virtual function call is the extra pointer dereferencing. A virtual function call usually executes as fast as or faster than the **switch** statement that would otherwise be used.

Pure Virtual Functions

In the example of the employee-database program, the Employee class defines a do-nothing computePay function. This solution is somewhat inelegant, because the function is intended never to be called.

A better solution is to declare computePay as a "pure virtual function." This is done by specifying an equal sign and a zero after the member function's prototype, as follows:

```
class Employee
{
public:
    // ...
    virtual double computePay() const = 0;  // Pure virtual
};
```

A pure virtual function requires no definition; you don't have to write the body of Employee::computePay. It is intended to be redefined in all derived classes. In the base class, the function serves no purpose except to provide a polymorphic interface for the derived classes.

You cannot declare any instances of a class in which a function is declared as pure virtual. For example, because computePay is now a pure virtual function, you cannot declare any objects of type Employee.

This restriction is necessary to prevent anyone from calling a pure virtual function for an object. If you could declare a generic Employee object, you could call computePay for it, which would be meaningless. You can only declare objects of the derived classes that provide a definition for computePay.

A class that defines pure virtual functions is known as an "abstract class," because you cannot declare any instances of it. (Classes that you can declare instances of are sometimes called "concrete classes.") It is legal, however, to declare pointers to an abstract class. For example, you can declare Employee pointers and use them for manipulating objects of derived classes. This is the way computePayroll and the other employee-database functions work.

If a derived class does not provide a definition for a pure virtual function, the function is inherited as pure virtual, and the derived class becomes an abstract class too. This does not happen with ordinary virtual functions, because when a derived class omits a definition of an ordinary virtual function, it uses the base class's version. With pure virtual functions, the derived class cannot use the base class's version because the base class doesn't have a version. Thus, if WageEmployee did not define a version of computePay, it would be an abstract class too.

It's common to write a class hierarchy consisting of one or more abstract classes at the top that act as base classes for the concrete classes at the bottom. You cannot derive an abstract class from a concrete class.

Sometimes it's useful to write an abstract class that has few or no data members or code, consisting primarily of pure virtual functions. Most of the data and the code for the functions is defined when a new class is derived from such a base class. This is desirable when the base class's interface embodies a set of properties or operations that you'd like many other classes to have, but the implementations of those properties or operations differ for each class.

For example, consider a SortedList class that can store objects of any class:

```
class SortedList
{
public:
    SortedList();
    void addItem( const SortableObject &newItem );
    // ...
private:
    // ...
};
```

A SortedList object stores pointers to objects of class SortableObject. This is an abstract class that has pure virtual functions named isEqual and isLessThan:

```
class SortableObject
{
public:
    virtual int isEqual( const SortableObject &other ) const = 0;
    virtual int isLessThan( const SortableObject &other ) const = 0;
};
```

If you want to store names in a SortedList, you can derive a class called SortableName from SortableObject. You can then implement isEqual and isLessThan to perform string comparisons. For example:

```
class SortableName : public SortableObject
{
public:
    int isEqual( const SortableObject &other ) const;
    int isLessThan( const SortableObject &other ) const;
private:
    char name[30];
};

int SortableName::isEqual( const SortableObject &other ) const
{
    return (strncmp( name, other.name, 30 ) == 0);
};

// Similar implementation for isLessThan
```

Similarly, if you want to store ZIP Codes, you can derive a class SortableZIP from SortableObject and implement the member functions to compare numbers. SortableObject thus provides a template for you to use when writing your own classes. By itself, SortableObject isn't a useful class, because it contains no code or data. You supply those when you derive a class from it.

Destructors in Base and Derived Classes

If destructors are defined for a base and a derived class, they are executed in the reverse order that the constructors are executed. When an object of a derived class goes out of scope, the destructor for the derived class is called and then the destructor for the base class is called.

When destroying dynamically created objects with the **delete** operator, a problem can arise. If **delete** is applied to a base class pointer, the compiler calls the base class destructor, even if the pointer points to an instance of a derived class.

The solution is to declare the base class's destructor as **virtual**. This causes the destructors of all derived classes to be virtual, even though they don't share the same name as the base class's destructor. Then if **delete** is applied to a base class pointer, the appropriate destructor is called, no matter what type of object the pointer is pointing to.

Notice that Employee has a virtual destructor, even though the destructor does nothing. Whenever you write a class that has virtual functions, you should always give it a virtual destructor, even if the class doesn't need one. The reason is that a derived class might require a destructor. For example, suppose you derive a class from `Employee` called `Consultant`, and that derived class defines a destructor. By defining a virtual destructor in the base class, you ensure that the derived class's destructor is called when needed.

Note that while destructor functions can be virtual, constructor functions cannot.

Protected Members

Besides the **public** and **private** keywords, C++ provides a third keyword controlling the visibility of a class's members: the **protected** keyword. Protected members are just like private members except that they are accessible to the member functions of derived classes.

As noted earlier, derived classes have no special privileges when it comes to accessing a class's private members. If you want to permit access by only the derived classes, and not by anyone else, you can declare some of your data members as **protected**. For example:

```
class Base
{
public:
protected:
    int secret;
private:
    int topSecret;
};

class Derived : public Base
{
public:
    void func();
};

void Derived::func()
{
    secret = 1;       // Can access protected member
    topSecret = 1;    // Error: Can't access private member
}
```

```
void main()
{
    Base aBase;
    Derived aDerived;

    aBase.secret = 1;       // Error: Can't access protected member
    aBase.topSecret = 1;    // Error: Can't access private member
    aDerived.secret = 1;    // Error: Can't access protected member
                            //        in derived class either
}
```

In this example, the private member `topSecret` is inaccessible to the derived class's member functions, but the protected member `secret` is accessible. However, the protected member is never accessible to outside functions.

Protected members in the base class are protected members in the derived class too. Functions using the derived class cannot access its protected members.

You should use the **protected** keyword with care. If the protected portion of a base class is rewritten, all the derived classes that used those protected members must be rewritten as well.

Public and Private Base Classes

The derived classes in this chapter all specify the keyword **public** in front of the base class's name. This specifies public derivation, which means that the public members of the base class are public members of the derived class, and protected members of the base class are protected members of the derived class.

You can also specify the keyword **private** in front of the base class's name. This specifies private derivation, which means that both the public and protected members of the base class are private members of the derived class. Those members are accessible to the derived class's member functions, but not to anyone using the derived class.

Private derivation is rarely used. Someone using the class cannot implicitly convert a pointer to a derived class object into a pointer to a base class object, or use polymorphism. (However, within the member functions of the derived class, you can perform such conversions and use polymorphism). Private derivation is very similar to defining a member object of another class; it's a method of using another class, but it's not appropriate for indicating that one class is a subtype of another.

Multiple Inheritance

The previous examples in this chapter demonstrate "single inheritance," where a class is derived from a single base class. C++ also supports "multiple inheritance," where a class can be derived from more than one base class.

For example, suppose you wanted to declare a class SalesManager to describe employees who have characteristics of both the SalesPerson and Manager classes:

```
class SalesManager : public SalesPerson, public Manager
{
// ...
};
```

The SalesManager class inherits all the data members and member functions of SalesPerson and Manager.

You cannot specify a class as a direct base class more than once (for example, you cannot enter Manager twice in the list of base classes). However, a class can be an indirect base class more than once. For example, SalesManager has Employee as an indirect base class twice: once through SalesPerson and once through Manager. As a result, each SalesManager object contains two copies of Employee's data members.

If a class acts as an indirect base class more than once, it is more complicated to call member functions defined by that base class. For example:

```
SalesManager aSellerBoss;
char *str;

str = aSellerBoss.getName();    // Error: ambiguous
```

The problem is that the compiler can't tell which copy of Employee should be used; because each copy's data members might contain different values, the value returned by getName depends on which copy is used. You must specify which copy you want, using the scope resolution operator:

```
str = aSellerBoss.Manager::getName();
```

This statement uses the name stored in the Manager's copy of Employee's data members.

The same ambiguity problem can arise even if an indirect base class is not repeated. If a base class (either direct or indirect) defines a member with the same name as a member defined in another base class, you must again use the scope resolution operator to specify whose member you want.

If a class acts as an indirect base more than once, there are also possible ambiguities when performing conversions between base and derived classes. For example, suppose you want to convert a pointer to a `SalesManager` into a pointer to an `Employee`:

```
Employee *empPtr;
SalesManager *salemgrPtr;

empPtr = salemgrPtr;    // Error: ambiguous
```

Once again, the compiler can't tell which copy of `Employee` it should use for `empPtr`. To disambiguate, you must use a cast:

```
empPtr = (Manager *)salemgrPtr;
```

This statement converts `salemgrPtr` into a pointer to a `Manager` and then converts that into a pointer to an `Employee`. As a result, `empPtr` points to `Manager`'s copy of `Employee`'s data members.

Because sales managers don't have two names and two social security numbers, the `SalesManager` class shouldn't contain two copies of `Employee`. To avoid this duplication, you can make `Employee` a "virtual base class."

To do this, the classes that specify `Employee` as a direct base class must use the **virtual** keyword:

```
class WageEmployee : public virtual Employee
{
    // ...
};

class Manager : public virtual Employee
{
    // ...
};
```

Note that only `WageEmployee` and `Manager` need to use the **virtual** keyword. `SalesPerson` and `SalesManager` do not, because `Employee` is an indirect base class for them.

By making `Employee` a virtual base class, each instance of `SalesManager` now has only one copy of `Employee`'s data members; there is no duplication. Any references to members defined by `Employee` are unambiguous, and so are conversions from a `SalesManager` pointer to a `Employee` pointer.

For a class like `SalesManager`, virtual base classes save space and allow a more accurate representation. However, virtual base classes impose a greater processing overhead. Consequently, you should use virtual base classes sparingly.

For information on design issues surrounding multiple inheritance, see Chapter 9, "Fundamentals of Object-Oriented Design." For more information on single inheritance, virtual functions, multiple inheritance, and virtual base classes, see the *C++ Language Reference* online.

Operator Overloading and Conversion Functions

Classes are useful for representing numeric data types that are not built into the language. This chapter covers two features of C++ that can make these classes behave more like the built-in types: operator overloading, which makes it possible for you to use operators with your classes, and conversion functions, which make it possible for you to convert between classes.

This chapter covers the following topics:

- Overloading operators as member functions
- Overloading operators as friend functions
- Constructors that perform conversions
- Conversion operators

Operator Overloading

Chapter 5, "Classes and Dynamic Memory Allocation," described how you can redefine the meaning of the assignment operator (=) when it is used to assign objects of a class you write. That was an example of operator overloading, and the assignment operator is the operator most commonly overloaded when writing classes.

You can overload other operators to make your code more readable. For example, suppose you needed a function that compares Date objects, to see if one comes before another. You can write a function called lessThan and use it as follows:

```
if( lessThan( myDate, yourDate ) )
    // ...
```

As an alternative, you can overload the less-than operator (<) to compare two Date objects. This would allow you to write an expression like the following:

```
if( myDate < yourDate )
    // ...
```

This format is more intuitive and convenient to use than the previous one.

You have already seen overloaded operators in many examples in the previous chapters. All of the example programs printed their output with the << operator, which is overloaded in the **iostream** class library.

Operator overloading is most useful when writing classes that represent numeric types. For example, scientific programs often use complex numbers—that is, numbers with a real and an imaginary component. You could write a class Complex to represent these numbers. To perform tasks such as adding and multiplying complex numbers, you could write functions with names like add and mult, but this often results in lengthy statements that are hard to understand. For example:

```
a = mult( mult( add( b, c ), add( d, e ) ), f );
```

Typing an equation in this format is tedious and error-prone, and reading an unfamiliar equation in this format is even more difficult.

A better alternative is to overload the + and * operators to work on Complex objects. This results in statements like this:

```
a = (b + c) * (d + e) * f;
```

This format is easier for both the programmer writing the equation and the programmer who reads it later.

Rules of Operator Overloading

You can overload any of the following operators:

Table 8.1   Overloadable Operators

+	–	*	/	%	^	&	|
~	!	,	=	<	>	<=	>=
++	—	<<	>>	==	!=	&&	||
+=	–=	*=	/=	%=	^=	&=	|=
<<=	>>=	[ ]	( )	–>	–>*	new	delete

The last two operators, **new** and **delete**, are the free store operators, which were described in Chapter 5, "Classes and Dynamic Memory Allocation." The last operator before those (–>*) is the pointer-to-member operator, which is described in the *C++ Language Reference* in Books Online.

Certain operators can be used as either binary or unary operators. For example, the – operator means subtraction when used as a binary operator and negation when used as a unary operator. You can overload such operators to have different meanings in their different usages.

You can use overloaded operators in ways that, if they were not overloaded, would be meaningless. Consider the following expression:

```
cout << "Hello";
```

If the << operator were not overloaded, this expression would left-shift **cout** a number of bits equal to the value of the pointer to the string. The compiler would generate a run-time error when trying to execute this statement. But the statement is syntactically legal, so you can write an overloaded operator function that executes when this statement appears. (For information on overloading the << and >> operators to make your classes work with streams, see the *iostream Reference* online.)

There are a number of restrictions on operator overloading:

- You cannot extend the language by inventing new operators. For example, you cannot create your own "exponentiation" operator using the characters **. Those characters do not form a legal operator in C or C++, and you cannot make them one. You must limit yourself to existing operators.

- You cannot change an operator's "arity," that is, the number of operands that it takes. For example, the logical-NOT operator (~) is a unary operator, meaning that it takes one operand. You cannot use it as a binary operator for built-in types, so you cannot overload it to act as a binary operator for your class. For example:

```
a = ~b;          // Legal
a = b ~ c;       // Error
```

- You cannot change an operator's precedence. For example, the multiplication operator has a higher precedence than the addition operator, so the multiplication is performed first when the following expression is evaluated:

```
a = b + c * d;    // Same as a = b + (c * d);
```

You cannot overload the * and + operators in such a way that the addition is performed first. You must use parentheses to alter the order of evaluation. For example:

```
a = (b + c) * d;   // Parentheses control evaluation
```

One consequence of this is that the operator you choose may not have the precedence appropriate for the meaning you give it. For example, the ^ operator might seem an appropriate choice to perform exponentiation, but its precedence is lower than that of addition, which could confuse people using it.

- You cannot change an operator's associativity. When an operand is between two operators that have the same precedence, it is grouped with one or the other depending on its associativity. For example, the addition and subtraction operators are both left-associative, so the following expression is evaluated from left to right:

```
a = b + c - d;    // Same as a = (b + c) - d;
```

You cannot overload the + and − operators in such a way that the subtraction is performed first. You must use parentheses to alter the order of evaluation. For example:

```
a = b + (c - d);   // Parentheses control evaluation
```

- You cannot change the way an operator works with built-in data types. For example, you cannot change the meaning of the + operator for integers.

- You cannot overload the following operators:

Operator	Definition
.	Class member operator
.*	Pointer-to-member operator
::	Scope resolution operator
?:	Conditional expression operator

C++ lets you overload any of the other operators. However, just because you can overload an operator doesn't necessarily mean it's a good idea.

When Not to Overload Operators

You should overload operators only when the meaning of the operator is clear and unambiguous. The arithmetic operators, for example + and *, are meaningful when applied to numeric classes, such as complex numbers, but not to everything. For example, consider overloading the + operator for Date objects:

```
laterDate = myDate + yourDate;    // Meaning?
```

It's anyone's guess what this statement means.

Many programmers overload the + operator for a String class to perform concatenation of two String objects. However, overloading relational operators for a String class might not be appropriate:

```
String myString( "John Smith" ),
      yourString( "JOHN SMITH" );

if( myString == yourString )    // True or false?
      // ...
```

A person reading this statement cannot tell whether the comparison being performed is case sensitive or not. You could define a separate function to control case sensitivity, but the combination might not be as clear as using named member functions.

Sometimes, an overloaded operator clearly suggests a particular meaning to one programmer but suggests a different meaning to another programmer. For example, consider having a class Set, where each object represents a collection of objects.

It would be useful to be able to calculate the "union" of two sets, that is, the set that contains the contents of both without duplications. Someone might pick the **&&** operator for this purpose. For example:

```
ourSet = mySet && yourSet;    // Clearly union
```

The programmer who wrote this statement might think it clearly indicates that ourSet contains everything in mySet combined with everything in yourSet. But another programmer might use the operator in the following way:

```
// Intersection or union?
targetSet = wealthySet && unmarriedSet;
```

Does targetSet contain everyone who is *both* wealthy and unmarried? Or does it contains everyone who is *either* wealthy or unmarried?

Too many overloaded operators, or even a few badly chosen operators, can make your programs exceedingly difficult to read. Don't use overloaded operators simply to make it easier for you to type in your programs. Other programmers may have to maintain your programs later on, and it's much more important that they be able to understand your code. Accordingly, choose your overloaded operators with great care, and use them sparingly.

Because numeric classes are usually the best candidates for operator overloading, let's consider how to overload arithmetic operators for such a class.

Overloading Operators for a Numeric Class

As an example of a numeric class, consider a class called Fraction, which stores a number as the ratio of two long integers. This is useful because many numbers cannot be expressed exactly in floating-point notation. For example, the quantity 1/3 is represented as 0.33333. The expression 1/3 + 1/3 + 1/3 should add up to 1, but represented in floating-point notation it adds up to 0.99999. Over the course of a lengthy calculation, this type of error is cumulative and can become quite significant. A Fraction class removes this type of error.

To add two Fraction objects, you can overload the + operator as follows:

```
// Overloading the + operator
#include <stdlib.h>
#include <math.h>
#include <iostream.h>
class Fraction
```

```
{
public:
    Fraction();
    Fraction( long num, long den );
    void display() const;
    Fraction operator+( const Fraction &second ) const;
private:
    static long gcf( long first, long second );
    long numerator,
         denominator;
};

// ----------- Default constructor
Fraction::Fraction()
{
    numerator = 0;
    denominator = 1;
}

// ----------- Constructor
Fraction::Fraction( long num, long den )
{
    int factor;

    if( den == 0 )
        den = 1;
    numerator = num;
    denominator = den;
    if( den < 0 )
    {
        numerator = -numerator;
        denominator = -denominator;
    }
    factor = gcf( num, den );
    if( factor > 1 )
    {
        numerator /= factor;
        denominator /= factor;
    }
}

// ----------- Function to print a Fraction
void Fraction::display() const
{
    cout << numerator << '/' << denominator;
}
```

```
// ----------- Overloaded + operator
Fraction Fraction::operator+( const Fraction &second ) const
{
    long factor,
         mult1,
         mult2;

    factor = gcf( denominator, second.denominator );
    mult1 = denominator / factor;
    mult2 = second.denominator / factor;

    return Fraction( numerator * mult2 + second.numerator * mult1,
                     denominator * mult2 );
}

// ----------- Greatest common factor
// computed using iterative version of Euclid's algorithm
long Fraction::gcf( long first, long second )
{
    int temp;

    first = labs( first );
    second = labs( second );

    while( second > 0 )
    {
        temp = first % second;
        first = second;
        second = temp;
    }

    return first;
}
```

A Fraction object is declared with two integers, the numerator and the denominator. The constructor checks that the denominator is nonzero and nonnegative and simplifies the fraction if possible. The class defines a private static function named gcf to calculate the greatest common factor of two numbers.

The following program uses the Fraction class and demonstrates the use of the overloaded **+** operator:

```
void main()
{
    Fraction a,
             b( 23, 11 ),
             c( 2, 3 );

    a = b + c;

    a.display();
    cout << endl;
}
```

The expression b + c is interpreted as b.operator+(c). The **operator+** function is called for the b object, using c as a parameter.

An overloaded operator doesn't have to have objects for both operands. You can add a Fraction and an integer as well by writing another function:

```
Fraction Fraction::operator+( long second ) const
{
    return Fraction( numerator + second * denominator,
                     denominator );
}
```

This permits statements like the following:

```
void main()
{
    Fraction a,
             b( 2, 3 );

    a = b + 1234;
}
```

However, you cannot write a statement like this:

```
a = 1234 + b;  // Error
```

Because **operator+** is defined as a member function, the previous statement is interpreted as follows:

```
a = (1234).operator+( b );  // Error
```

This statement is clearly an error, because an integer doesn't have a member function that can be invoked to perform the addition.

To allow expressions where a variable of a built-in type is the first operand, you must use friend functions (described in Chapter 6, "More Features of Classes").

Defining Operators as Friend Functions

To overload an operator using a nonmember function, you define a function named **operator+** that takes two arguments, as follows:

```
class Fraction
{
public:
    Fraction( long num, long den );
    Fraction operator+( const Fraction &second ) const;
    Fraction operator+( long second ) const;
    friend Fraction operator+( long first,
                               const Fraction &second );
// ...
};

// ...

Fraction operator+( long first, const Fraction &second )
{
    return Fraction( second.numerator + first * second.denominator,
                     second.denominator );
}
```

With a function like this, an expression like this

```
a = 1234 + b;    // Friend function called
```

is interpreted as follows:

```
a = operator+( 1234, b );    // Friend function called
```

Notice that the friend function requires two parameters while the member function requires only one. The + operator requires two operands. When **operator+** is defined as a member function, the first operand is the object for which it is called, and the second the parameter. In contrast, when **operator+** is defined as a friend function, both operands are parameters to the function. You cannot define a friend and a member function that define the same operator, unless you distinguish them through their parameter lists.

You can also use either a member function or a friend function to implement a unary operator. For example, suppose you want to implement the negation (–) operator. You could do it as a member function that takes no parameters:

```
inline Fraction Fraction::operator-() const
{
    return Fraction( -numerator, denominator );
}
```

You could also implement it as a friend function that takes one parameter:

```
inline Fraction operator-( Fraction &one )
{
    return Fraction( -one.numerator, one.denominator );
}
```

When you overload an operator using a friend function, you must make at least one of the function's parameters an object. That is, you cannot write a binary **operator+** function that takes two integers as parameters. This prevents you from redefining the meaning of operators for built-in types.

Notice that you have to define three separate functions to handle the addition of Fraction objects and long integers. If you overload other arithmetic operators, such as * or /, you must also provide three functions for each operator. A technique for avoiding multiple versions of each operator is described in the section "Class Conversions."

Tips for Overloading Arithmetic Operators

Overloading the + operator does not mean that the += operator is overloaded. You must overload that operator separately. If you do, make sure that the normal identity relationships are maintained, that is, a += b has the same effect as a = a + b.

If you're overloading operators for a class whose objects are relatively large, you should pass parameters as references rather than by value. Also, be sure to pass references to constants, which allows constant objects to be operands.

The return type of an overloaded operator depends on the specific operator. Overloaded + or * operators for the Fraction class must return Fraction objects. Operators such as += and *=, on the other hand, can return references to Fraction objects for efficiency. This is because + and * create temporary objects containing new values, and they cannot return references to objects created within the function. In contrast, += and *= modify an existing object, ***this**, so they can safely return references to that object. (Recall that the overloaded = operator, described in Chapter 5, "Classes and Dynamic Memory Allocation," also returns a reference to an object.)

Overloading Operators for an Array Class

The array mechanism that is built into C is very primitive; it is essentially an alternate syntax for using pointers. An array doesn't store its size, and there is no way to keep someone from accidentally indexing past the end of the array. In C++, you can define a much safer and more powerful array type using a class. To make such a class look more like an array, you can overload the subscript operator ([ ]).

The following example defines the `IntArray` class, where each object contains an array of integers. This class overloads the [ ] operator to perform range checking.

```cpp
// Overloaded [] operator
#include <iostream.h>
#include <string.h>

class IntArray
{
public:
    IntArray( int len );
    int getLength() const;
    int &operator[]( int index );
    ~IntArray();
private:
    int length;
    int *aray;
};

// ------------ Constructor
IntArray::IntArray( int len )
{
    if( len > 0 )
    {
        length = len;
        aray = new int[len];
        // initialize contents of array to zero
        memset( aray, 0, sizeof( int ) * len );
    }
    else
    {
        length = 0;
        aray = 0;
    }
}

// ------------ Function to return length
inline int IntArray::getLength() const
{
    return length;
}
```

```
// ----------- Overloaded subscript operator
// Returns a reference
int &IntArray::operator[]( int index )
{
    static int dummy = 0;

    if( (index = 0) &&
        (index < length) )
        return aray[index];
    else
    {
        cout << "Error: index out of range.\n";
        return dummy;
    }
}

// ----------- Destructor
IntArray::~IntArray()
{
    delete aray;
}

void main()
{
    IntArray numbers( 10 );
    int i;

    for( i = 0; i < 10; i++ )
        numbers[i] = i;          // Use numbers[i] as lvalue

    for( i = 0; i < 10; i++ )
        cout << numbers[i] << '\n';
}
```

This program first declares an IntArray object that can hold 10 integers. Then it assigns a value to each element in the array. Notice that the array expression appears on the left side of the assignment. This is legal because the **operator[ ]** function returns a reference to an integer. Because the expression numbers[i] acts as an alias for an element in the private array, it can be the recipient of an assignment statement. In this situation, returning a reference is not simply more efficient—it is necessary.

The **operator[ ]** function checks whether the specified index value is within range or not. If it is, the function returns a reference to the corresponding element in the private array. If it isn't, the function prints out an error message and returns a reference to a static integer. This prevents out-of-range array references from overwriting other regions of memory, though it will probably cause unexpected program behavior. As an alternative, you could have the **operator[ ]** function exit the program when it receives an out-of-range index value.

As it is currently implemented, the index values for an IntArray object of size *n* range from 0 to *n*–1, but that is not a requirement. You can use any value you want for the bounds of the array or even have the bounds specified when an object is declared.

The IntArray class has a number of advantages over conventional arrays in C. The size of an IntArray doesn't have to be a constant; you can determine the size at run time without having to use the **new** and **delete** operators. An IntArray object also stores its size, so you can pass one to a function without having to pass the size separately. One possible enhancement is to make IntArray objects resizable, so that you could expand one if it became full.

You can also overload **operator[ ]** for classes that aren't implemented as arrays. For example, you could write a linked list class and allow users to use array notation to access the nodes in the list. You can even use values other than integers for indexing. For example, consider the following prototype:

```
int &operator[]( const char *key );
```

This **operator[ ]** function takes a string as an index. This permits expressions like the following:

```
salary["John Smith"] = 25000;
```

You could use the string as a key for searching through a data structure, which could be an array or a linked list or something else. Because it would be difficult to iterate through such a class using a **for** loop, this class would probably benefit from having an iterator implemented with a friend class, as mentioned in Chapter 6, "More Features of Classes."

The **operator[ ]** function takes only one parameter. You cannot give it multiple parameters to simulate a multidimensional array. For example:

```
int &SquareArray::operator[]( int row, int col );  // Error
```

You can, however, overload the () operator, which can take an arbitrary number of parameters. For example:

```
int &SquareArray::operator()( int row, int col );
```

This allows statements like the following:

```
SquareArray myArray;

myArray( 3, 4 ) = 1;
```

Note that this is not standard array notation in C, so it may be confusing for other programmers reading your code.

The **operator[ ]** function cannot be defined as a friend function. It must be a nonstatic member function.

Class Conversions

Both C and C++ have a set of rules for converting one type to another. These rules are used in the following situations:

- When assigning a value. For example, if you assign an integer to an variable of type **long**, the compiler converts the integer to a long.

- When performing an arithmetic operation. For example, if you add an integer and a floating-point value, the compiler converts the integer to a double before it performs the addition.

- When passing an argument to a function—for example, if you pass an integer to a function that expects a long.

- When returning a value from a function—for example, if you return an integer from a function that has **double** as its return type.

In all of these situations, the compiler performs the conversion implicitly. You can make the conversion explicit by using a cast expression.

When you define a class in C++, you can specify the conversions that the compiler can apply when you use instances of that class. You can define conversions between classes, or between a class and a built-in type.

Conversion by Constructor

Chapter 4, "Introduction to Classes," described constructors, the functions that create objects. A constructor that takes only one parameter is considered a conversion function; it specifies a conversion from the type of the parameter to the type of the class. For example, suppose you specify a default value for the denominator parameter of the Fraction constructor, as follows:

```
class Fraction
{
public:
    Fraction( long num, long den = 1 );
    // ...
};
```

This constructor not only lets you initialize a Fraction object using only one number, it also lets you assign integers to a Fraction object directly. For example:

```
Fraction a( 2 );    // Equivalent to Fraction a( 2 , 1 );

a = 7;          // Equivalent to a = Fraction( 7 );
                //                a = Fraction( 7, 1 );
```

In the above statement, the compiler uses the single-argument constructor to implicitly convert an integer into a temporary Fraction object and then uses the object for the assignment. Similarly, if you pass an integer to a function that expects a Fraction object, the integer is converted before the function is called.

To be more precise, when you pass the Fraction constructor an integer, the compiler actually performs a standard conversion and a user-defined conversion at once. For example:

```
a = 7;    // int -> long -> Fraction
```

The compiler first performs a standard conversion to make the integer into a long integer. Then it converts the long integer into a Fraction and performs the assignment.

One result of defining an implicit conversion is that one operator function can handle several different types of expressions. Suppose you define just one **operator+** function for the Fraction class:

```
class Fraction
{
public:
    Fraction( long num, long den = 1 );
    friend Fraction operator+( const Fraction &first,
                               const Fraction &second );
    // ...
};
```

The combination of that constructor and that operator function accepts all of these expressions:

```
Fraction a,
        b( 2, 3 ),
        c( 4, 5 );

a = b + c;          // Okay as is
a = b + 1234;       // a = b + Fraction( 1234 );
a = 1234 + b;       // a = Fraction( 1234 ) + b;
a = 1234 + 5678;    // a = Fraction( 6912 );
```

When the compiler evaluates each expression, it looks for an **operator+** function that fits. If it can't find one, it tries to convert one or more of the operands so that they match the **operator+** function that does exist. As a result, the compiler converts the integers into Fraction objects and performs the addition on them.

Notice that in the last assignment statement the compiler does not convert the integers into Fraction objects. It is able to add the integers directly. The compiler then converts the resulting sum into a temporary Fraction object to perform the assignment.

A single-argument constructor defines an implicit conversion that turns instances of other types into objects of your class, so that your class is the *target* of the conversion. You can also define an implicit conversion that turns objects of your class into instances of other types, making your class the *source* of the conversion. To do this, you define a "conversion operator."

Conversion Operators

Suppose you want to be able to pass a Fraction object to a function that expects a **double**—that is, you want to convert Fraction objects into floating-point values. The following example defines a conversion operator to do just that:

```
// Conversion member function
#include <iostream.h>

class Fraction
{
public:
    Fraction( long num, long den = 1 );
    operator double() const;
    // ...
};

Fraction::operator double() const
{
    return (double)numerator / (double)denominator;
}
```

The function operator double converts a Fraction object to a floating-point value. Notice that the operator function has no return type and takes no parameters. A conversion operator must be a nonstatic member function; you cannot define it as a friend function.

You can call the conversion operator using one of several syntax variations:

```
Fraction a;
double f;

f = a.operator double();  // Convert using explicit call
f = double( a );          // Convert using constructor syntax
f = (double)a;            // Convert using cast syntax
f = a;                    // Convert implicitly
```

The compiler can perform a standard conversion and a user-defined conversion at once. For example:

```
Fraction a( 123, 12 );
int i;

i = a;  // Fraction -> double -> integer
```

The compiler first converts the `Fraction` object into a floating-point number. Then it performs a standard conversion, making the floating-point number into an integer, and performs the assignment.

A conversion operator doesn't have to convert from a class to a built-in type. You can also use a conversion operator that converts one class into another. For example, suppose you had defined the numeric class `FixedPoint` to store fixed-point numbers. You could define a conversion operator as follows:

```
class Fraction
{
public:
    operator FixedPoint() const;
};
```

This operator would permit implicit conversions of a `Fraction` object into a `FixedPoint` object.

Conversion operators are useful for defining an implicit conversion from your class to a class whose source code you don't have access to. For example, if you want a conversion from your class to a class that resides within a library, you cannot define a single-argument constructor for that class. Instead, you must use a conversion operator.

Ambiguities with Conversions and Operators

The inclusion of the `operator double` conversion operator creates problems for the `Fraction` class. Consider the following statement:

```
a = b + 1234;   // Error: ambiguous
                //     a = (double)b + 1234;
                //     a = b + Fraction( 1234 );
```

The compiler could either convert b to a floating-point number and then add that together with the integer, or it could convert 1234 to a `Fraction` and then add the two `Fraction` objects. That is, the compiler could add the two values as built-in types, or it could add them as objects. The compiler has no basis for choosing one conversion over the other, so it generates an error.

There are several ways you could modify the Fraction class to resolve this ambiguity. One is to use an ordinary member function to perform addition, instead of overloading the + operator. For example:

```
class Fraction
{
    friend Fraction add( const Fraction &first,
                          const Fraction &second );
};
```

Because this function does not look like the + operator, there is no confusion between adding two values as Fraction objects or adding them as built-in types.

Another solution is to remove an implicit conversion. You could remove the implicit conversion from an integer to a Fraction by getting rid of the single-argument constructor. This requires you to rewrite the previous statement as:

```
a = b + Fraction( 1234, 1 );
```

If you wanted to add the values as built-in types, you'd write the following:

```
a = (double)b + 1234;
```

Or you could remove the implicit conversion from a Fraction to a floating-point number, by changing the conversion operator into an ordinary member function. For example:

```
class Fraction
{
public:
    double cvtToFloat() const;
    // ...
};
```

This leaves only one interpretation for the following statement:

```
a = b + 1234;      // a = b + Fraction( 1234 );
```

If you wanted to add the two values as built-in types, you'd write the following:

```
a = b.cvtToFloat() + 1234;
```

If you wish to retain the convenience of both of these implicit conversions, as well as use operator overloading, you must explicitly define multiple versions of the **operator+** function:

```
class Fraction
{
    friend Fraction operator+( const Fraction &first,
                                const Fraction &second );
    friend Fraction operator+( int first,
                                const Fraction &second );
    friend Fraction operator+( const Fraction &first,
                                int second );
    // more...
};
```

If the appropriate functions are defined, the compiler doesn't have to perform any conversions to resolve expressions that mix Fraction objects and integers. The compiler simply calls the function that matches each possibility. This solution requires more work when writing the class, but it makes the class more usable.

As this example illustrates, you must use considerable care if you define both overloaded operators and implicit conversions.

Ambiguities Between Conversions

An ambiguity can arise when two classes define the same conversion. For example:

```
class FixedPoint;

class Fraction
{
public:
    Fraction( FixedPoint value );   // FixedPoint -> Fraction
};

class FixedPoint
{
public:
    operator Fraction();            // FixedPoint -> Fraction
};
void main()
{
    Fraction a;
    FixedPoint b;

    a = b;          // Error; ambiguous
                    //     a = Fraction( b );
                    //     a = b.operator Fraction();
}
```

The compiler cannot choose between the constructor and the conversion operator. You can explicitly specify the conversion operator, but not the constructor:

```
a = b.operator Fraction();      // Call conversion operator
a = Fraction( b );              // Error: still ambiguous
a = (Fraction)b;                // Error: still ambiguous
```

This type of ambiguity is easy to avoid, because it occurs only when the classes know of each other, which means that they were written by the same programmer(s). If you simply remove one of the conversion functions, the problem does not arise.

Ambiguities can also arise when multiple classes define similar implicit conversions. For example, suppose you have the Fraction class and some associated functions that use Fraction objects, as follows:

```
class Fraction
{
public:
    Fraction( double value );      // double -> Fraction
};

void calc( Fraction parm );
```

You might also have a FixedPoint class that includes a similar set of associated functions:

```
class FixedPoint
{
public:
    FixedPoint( double value );    // double -> FixedPoint
};

void calc( FixedPoint parm );
```

Now consider what happens if you try to use both the Fraction and the FixedPoint classes in the same program:

```
void main()
{
    calc( 12.34 ); // Error: ambiguous
                   //     calc( Fraction( 12.34 ) );
                   //     calc( FixedPoint( 12.34 ) );
}
```

The compiler cannot choose which conversion to apply when calling the `calc` function. This type of ambiguity is difficult to avoid, because it can occur even if `Fraction` and `FixedPoint` are written by different programmers. Neither programmer would have noticed the problem because it doesn't appear when either class is used by itself; the ambiguity arises only when they are used together. This problem can be solved if the user of the classes explicitly specifies a conversion by using the constructor for the class desired.

It is difficult to anticipate all possible ambiguities that may involve your class. When you write a class, you might define only a small number of conversions. However, when other programmers write their classes, they can also define conversions involving your class. They can define constructors that convert an object of your class into an object of one of theirs, or they can define conversion operators that turn an object of one of their classes into an object of one of your classes.

To reduce the likelihood of ambiguities, you should define implicit conversions for your classes only when there is a clear need for them. You can always perform conversions explicitly by using constructors that require more than one argument, or by using ordinary member functions to perform conversions (for example, `cvtToOtherType`).

See the *C++ Language Reference* online for a complete description of the rules governing conversions.

Object-Oriented Design

Fundamentals of Object-Oriented Design

The preceding chapters covered the basic syntax of the C++ language. This chapter discusses object-oriented programming, the style of programming that C++ is designed to support.

The first section of this chapter, Features of Object-Oriented Programming, discusses the major concepts of object-oriented programming. The remainder of this chapter outlines the process of designing an object-oriented program.

Features of Object-Oriented Programming

In the traditional, procedure-oriented view of programming, a program describes a series of steps to be performed—that is, an algorithm. In the object-oriented view of programming, a program describes a system of objects interacting. It's possible to use C++ as a strictly procedural language. An object-oriented approach, however, lets you take full advantage of C++'s features.

Object-oriented programming involves a few key concepts. The most basic of these is abstraction, which makes writing large programs simpler. Another is encapsulation, which makes it easier to change and maintain a program. Finally, there is the concept of class hierarchies, a powerful classification tool that can make a program easily extensible. While you can apply these concepts using any language, object-oriented languages have been specifically designed to support them explicitly.

Abstraction

"Abstraction" is the process of ignoring details in order to concentrate on essential characteristics. A programming language is traditionally considered "high-level" if it supports a high degree of abstraction. For example, consider two programs that perform the same task, one written in assembly language, one in C.

The assembly-language program contains a very detailed description of what the computer does to perform the task, but programmers usually aren't concerned with what happens at that level. The C program gives a much more abstract description of what the computer does, and that abstraction makes the program clearer and easier to understand.

While traditional languages support abstraction, object-oriented languages provide much more powerful abstraction mechanisms. To understand how, consider the different types of abstraction.

Procedural Abstraction

The most common form of abstraction is "procedural abstraction," which lets you ignore details about processes.

There are many levels of procedural abstraction. For example, it's possible to describe what a program does in even greater detail than assembly language does, by listing the individual steps that the CPU performs when executing each assembly language instruction. On the other hand, a program written in the macro language of an application program can describe a given task on a much higher level than C does.

When you write a program in a given language, you aren't restricted to using the level of abstraction that the language itself provides. Most languages allow you to write programs at a higher level of procedural abstraction, by supporting user-defined functions (also known as procedures or subroutines). By writing your own functions, you define new terms to express what your program does.

As a simple example of procedural abstraction, consider a program that frequently has to check whether two strings are the same, ignoring case:

```
while (*s != '\0')
{
    if ( (*s == *t) ||
        ((*s >= 'A') && (*s <= 'Z') && ((*s + 32) == *t)) ||
        ((*t >= 'A') && (*t <= 'Z') && ((*t + 32) == *s))   )
    {
        s++; t++;
    }
    else break;
}
if ( *s == '\0' )
    printf("equal \n");
else
    printf("not equal \n");
```

By writing a program this way, you are constantly reminded of the comparisons that the program performs to check whether two strings are equal. An alternate way to write this program is to place the string comparison in a function:

```
if ( !_stricmp( s, t ) )
    printf("equal \n");
else
    printf("not equal \n");
```

The use of **_stricmp** does more than save you a lot of typing. It also makes the program easier to understand, because it hides details that can distract you. The precise steps performed by the function aren't important. What's important is that a case-insensitive string comparison is being performed.

Functions make large programs easier to design by letting you think in terms of logical operations, rather than in specific statements of the programming language.

Data Abstraction

Another type of abstraction is "data abstraction," which lets you ignore details of how a data type is represented.

For example, all computer data can be viewed as hexadecimal or binary numbers. However, because most programmers prefer to think in terms of decimal numbers, most languages support integer and floating-point data types. You can simply type "3.1416" rather than some hexadecimal bytes. Similarly, Basic provides a string data type, which lets you perform operations on strings intuitively, ignoring the details of how they're represented. On the other hand, C does not support the abstraction of strings, because the language requires you to manipulate strings as series of characters occupying consecutive memory locations.

Data abstraction always involves some degree of procedural abstraction as well. When you perform operations on variables of a given data type, you don't know the format of the data, so you can ignore the details of how operations are performed on those data types. How floating-point arithmetic is performed in binary is, thankfully, something C programmers don't have to worry about.

Compared to their capacity for procedural abstraction, most languages have very limited support for creating new levels of data abstraction. C supports user-defined data types through structures and **typedef**s. Most programmers use structures as no more than aggregates of variables. For example:

```
struct PersonInfo
{
    char name[30];
    long phone;
    char address1[30];
    char address2[30];
};
```

Such a user-defined type is convenient because it lets you manipulate several pieces of information as a unit instead of individually. However, this type doesn't provide any conceptual advantage. There's no point in thinking about the structure without thinking about the three pieces of information it contains.

A better example of data abstraction is the **FILE** type defined in STDIO.H:

```
typedef struct _iobuf
{
    char --far *_ptr;
    int _cnt;
    char --far *_base;
    char _flag;
    char _file;
} FILE;
```

A **FILE** structure is conceptually much more than the fields contained within it. You can think about **FILE**s without knowing how they're represented. You simply use a **FILE** pointer with various library functions, and let them handle the details.

Notice that it's possible to declare a structure without declaring the functions needed to use the structure. The C language lets you view data abstraction and procedural abstraction as two distinct techniques, when in fact they're integrally linked.

Classes

This is where object-oriented programming comes in. Object-oriented languages combine procedural and data abstraction, in the form of classes. When you define a class, you describe everything about a high-level entity at once. When using an object of that class, you can ignore the built-in types contained in the class and the procedures used to manipulate them.

Consider a simple class: polygonal shapes. You might think of a polygon as a series of points, which can be stored as a series of paired numbers. However, a polygon is conceptually much more than the sum of its vertices. A polygon has a perimeter, an area, and a characteristic shape. You might want to move one, rotate it, or reflect it. Given two polygons, you might want to find their intersection or their union or see if their shapes are identical. All of these properties and operations are perfectly meaningful without reference to any low-level entities that might make up a polygon. You can think about polygons without thinking about the numbers that might be stored in a polygon object, and without thinking about the algorithms for manipulating them.

With support for combined data abstraction and procedural abstraction, object-oriented languages make it easy for you to create an additional layer of separation between your program and the computer. The high-level entities you define have the same advantage that floating-point numbers and **printf** statements have when compared to bytes and **MOV** instructions: They make it easier to write long and complex applications.

Classes can also represent entities that you usually wouldn't consider data types. For example, a class can represent a binary tree. Each object is not simply a node in a tree, the way a C structure is; each object is a tree in itself. It's just as easy to create multiple binary trees as it is to create one. More importantly, you can ignore all the nonessential details of a binary tree. What features of a binary tree are you really interested in? The ability to quickly search for an item, to add or delete items, and to enumerate all the items in sorted order. It really doesn't matter what data structure you use, as long as you can perform the same set of operations on it. It might be a tree implemented with nodes and pointers, or a tree implemented with an array, or some data structure you've never heard of.

Such a class shouldn't be called `BinaryTree`, because that name implies a particular implementation. Based on the operations that can be performed on it, the class should be called `SortedList` or something similar.

By designing your program around abstract entities that have their own set of operations, rather than using data structures made of built-in types, you make your program more independent from implementation details. This leads to another advantage of object-oriented programming: encapsulation.

Encapsulation

"Encapsulation," which was mentioned in Chapter 4, "Introduction to Classes," is the process of hiding the internal workings of a class to support or enforce abstraction. This requires drawing a sharp distinction between a class's "interface," which has public visibility, and its "implementation," which has private visibility. A class's interface describes what a class can do, while its implementation describes how it does it. This distinction supports abstraction by exposing only the relevant properties of a class; a user views an object in terms of the operations it can perform, not in terms of its data structure.

Sometimes encapsulation is defined as the act of combining functions and data, but this is slightly misleading. You can join functions and data together in a class and make all the members public, but that is not an example of encapsulation. A truly encapsulated class "surrounds" or hides its data with its functions, so that you can access the data only by calling the functions. This is illustrated in Figure 9.1.

Figure 9.1   Hiding Data with Functions

Object with public data members

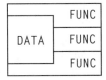

Object with private data members

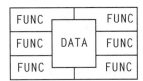

Encapsulation is not unique to object-oriented programming. The principle of "data hiding" in traditional structured programming is the same idea applied to modules rather than classes. It is common practice to divide a large program into modules, each of which has a clearly defined interface of functions that the other modules can use. The aim of data hiding is to make each module as independent of one another as possible. Ideally, a module has no knowledge of the data structures used by other modules, and it refers to those modules only through their interfaces. The use of global variables or data structures is kept to a minimum to limit the opportunity for modules to affect one another.

For example, suppose a program needs to maintain a table of information. All the functions acting on the table could be defined in one module, the file TABLE.C, and their prototypes could be declared in a file called TABLE.H:

```
/* TABLE.H */
#include "record.h"    /* Get definition of RECORD data type */

void add_item( RECORD *new_item );
RECORD *search_item( char *key );
.
.
.
```

If any function in the program needs to use the table, it calls one of the functions defined in TABLE.H. The TABLE.C module might implement the table as an array, but the other modules don't know about it. If that array is declared **static**, it is actually inaccessible outside of TABLE.C. Only the interface is visible then, while the implementation is completely hidden.

Data hiding provides a number of benefits. One of them is abstraction, which was described previously; you can use a module without having to think about how it works. Another is "locality," which means that changes to one part of the program don't require changes to the other parts. A program with poor locality is very fragile; modifying one section causes other sections to break, because they all depend on one another. A program with good locality is stable and easier to maintain; the effects of a change are confined to a small portion of the program. If you change the array in TABLE.C to a linked list or some other data structure, you don't have to rewrite any module that uses the table.

Hiding data within a module has its limitations. In the example mentioned above, the TABLE module does not permit you to have more than one table of information in your program, nor does it let you declare a table that is local to a particular function. You can gain these capabilities by using structures and pointers. For example, you could use pointers as handles to tables and write functions that take a table pointer as a parameter:

```
/* TABLE.H */
#include "record.h"

/* define TABLE with a typedef */

TABLE *create_table();
void add_item( TABLE *handle, RECORD *new_item );
RECORD *search_item( TABLE *handle, char *key );
void *destroy_table( TABLE *handle );
```

This technique is considerably more powerful than that used in the previous example. It lets you use multiple tables at once and have separate tables for different functions. However, the TABLE type provided by this module cannot be used as easily as built-in data types. For example, local tables are not automatically destroyed upon exit from a function. Like dynamically allocated variables, these tables require extra programming effort to be used properly.

Now consider the corresponding implementation in C++:

```
// TABLE.H
#include "record.h"

class Table
{
public:
    Table();
    void addItem( Record *newItem );
    Record *searchItem( char *key );
    ~Table();
private:
    //...
};
    .
    .
    .

// PROG.CPP
#include "table.h"

void func()
{
    Table first, second;

    //...
}
```

This class has two advantages over the technique of using table handles in C. The first one, as mentioned earlier, is ease of use. You can declare instances of `Table` the same way you declare integers or floating-point numbers, and the same scoping rules apply to all of them.

Second, and more important, the class enforces encapsulation. In the technique using table pointers, it is only a matter of convention that programmers do not access what's behind the table handle. Many programmers may choose to circumvent the interface of functions and manipulate a table directly. If the implementation of a table changes, it's very time consuming to locate every place in the source code where the programmer's assumptions about the data structure are now invalid. Such errors might not be detected by the compiler and might remain undetected until run time, when (for example) a null pointer is dereferenced and the program fails. Even minor changes to the implementation can create such problems. Sometimes the changes are intended to correct bugs but instead cause new ones because other functions depend on the specifics of an implementation.

In contrast, by declaring `Table` as a class, you can use the access rules of C++ to hide the implementation. You don't have to rely on the self-restraint of programmers who use your class. Any program that attempts to access the private data of a `Table` object won't compile. This makes it much more likely that locality will be maintained.

A common reason programmers break convention and access a data structure directly is that they can easily perform an operation that is cumbersome to do using only the functions in the interface. A well-designed class interface can minimize this problem if it reflects the important properties of the class. While no interface can make all possible operations convenient, it's usually best to forbid access to a class's internal data structure, even if it means an occasional piece of inefficient code. The minor loss in convenience is far outweighed by the increased maintainability of the program that encapsulation provides. By eliminating the need to modify most of the modules in a large program whenever a change is made, object-oriented languages can dramatically reduce the time and effort needed to develop new systems or update existing ones.

Even if the class interface changes in the future, it is still a good idea to use an encapsulated class rather than accessible data structures. In most cases, the changes to the interface can be formulated solely as additions to the existing interface, providing for upward compatibility. Any code that uses the old interface still works correctly. The code has to be recompiled, but that involves only computer time, not programmer time.

Note that, in C++, encapsulation does not provide a guarantee of safety. A programmer who is intent on using a class's private data can always use the **&** and * operators to gain access to them. Encapsulation simply protects against *casual* use of a class's internal representation.

Class Hierarchies

One feature of object-oriented programming that is not found at all in procedural programming is the ability to define a hierarchy of types. In C++, you can define one class as a subtype, or special category, of another class by deriving it from that class. You can also express similarities between classes, or define them as subcategories of a single broad category, by deriving them all from one base class. By contrast, the C language treats all types as completely independent of one another.

Identifying a common base class for several classes is a form of abstraction. A base class is a high-level way to view those classes. It specifies what the derived classes have in common, so you can concentrate on those shared traits and ignore their individual characteristics. This abstraction technique lets you view entities in terms of a small number of categories instead of a large number. This technique is often used in everyday thinking; for example, it's easier to think "mammals" instead of "lions, tigers, bears..." and "bears" rather than "grizzly bears, black bears, polar bears...."

Whereas a base class is a *generalization* of a group of classes, a derived class is a *specialization* of another class. A derived class identifies a subtype of a previously recognized type and describes it in terms of its additional characteristics. For example, lions are mammals, but they also have certain traits not found in all mammals.

There are two practical benefits of defining a class hierarchy: The derived class can share the base class's code, or it can share the base class's interface. These two benefits are not mutually exclusive, though a hierarchy designed for code reuse often has different characteristics from one designed to give a common interface.

Inheriting Code

If you are writing a class and want to incorporate the functionality of an existing class, you can simply derive your class from the existing one. This is a situation in which inheritance allows code reuse. For example, the `SalesPerson` class in Chapter 7, "Inheritance and Polymorphism," incorporated the functionality of the `WageEmployee` class.

If you're implementing several classes at once that share features, a class hierarchy can reduce redundant coding. You can describe and implement those common features just once in a base class, rather than repeatedly in each derived class.

For example, consider a program for designing data entry forms, where users fill out fields on-screen. The program allows forms to contain fields that accept names, fields that accept dates, fields that accept monetary values, and so forth. Each field accepts only the appropriate type of data. You could make each type of field a separate class, with names such as `NameField`, `DateField`, and `MoneyField`, each with its own criteria for validating input. Note that all the fields share some functionality. Each field is accompanied by a description telling the user what's requested, and the procedure for defining and displaying that description is the same for all fields. As a result, all the classes have identical implementations for their `setPrompt`, `displayPrompt`, and other functions.

You can save yourself effort as well as reduce the size of the program by defining a base class called `Field` that implements those functions. The `NameField`, `DateField`, and `MoneyField` classes can be derived from `Field` and inherit those functions. Such a class hierarchy also reduces the effort required to fix bugs or add features, because the changes have to be made only in one place.

A class hierarchy designed for code sharing has most of its code in the base classes (near the top of the hierarchy). This way, the code can be reused by many classes. The derived classes represent specialized or extended versions of the base class.

Inheriting an Interface

Another inheritance strategy is for a derived class to inherit just the names of its base class's member functions, not the code; the derived class provides its own code for those functions. The derived class thus has the same interface as the base class but performs different things with the same functions.

This strategy lets different classes use the same interface, thus reinforcing the high-level similarity in their behavior. However, the main benefit of inheriting an interface is polymorphism, which was exhibited by the Employee class in Chapter 7, "Inheritance and Polymorphism." All the classes derived from Employee shared its interface, making it possible to manipulate them as generic Employee objects.

In the example of the data entry forms, Field has a member function called getValue, but the function doesn't do anything useful. NameField inherits that member function and provides it with code to validate input as a legal name. DateField and MoneyField do the same, each providing different code for the function. Thus, individual field objects may have various types and exhibit different behaviors, but they all share the same interface and can all be treated as field objects.

A data entry form can simply maintain a list of field objects and ignore the distinctions between types of fields. To read values into all the fields, a form can iterate through its list of fields and call getValue for each without even knowing what types of fields are defined. The individual fields automatically get input using their own versions of getValue.

The example of the data entry forms uses inheritance for both code sharing and interface sharing. However, you can also design a class strictly for interface sharing by writing an abstract base class. The SortableObject class in Chapter 7 is an example of a class designed for pure interface sharing. The class's interface describes the necessary properties for an object to be stored in a SortedList object. However, the SortableObject class contains no code itself.

A class hierarchy designed for interface sharing has most of its code in the derived classes (near the bottom of the hierarchy). The derived classes represent working versions of an abstract model defined by the base class.

In summary, classes provide support for abstraction, encapsulation, and hierarchies. Classes are a mechanism for defining an abstract data type along with all the accompanying operations. Classes can be encapsulated, compartmentalizing your program and increasing its locality. Lastly, classes can be organized into hierarchies, highlighting their relationships to each other while letting you minimize redundant coding.

To gain the most benefit from object-oriented programming, you must do more than simply write your program in C++. The next section describes how you actually design an object-oriented program.

Designing an Object-Oriented System

In top-down structured programming, the first design step is to specify the program's intended function. You must answer the question, "What does the program do?" First you describe the major steps that the program must perform, using high-level pseudocode or flowcharts, and then you refine that description by breaking each major step into smaller ones. This technique is known as "procedural decomposition." It treats a program as a description of a process and breaks it down into subprocesses.

Object-oriented design differs dramatically from this technique. In object-oriented design, you don't analyze a problem in terms of tasks or processes. Nor do you describe it in terms of data; you don't begin by asking "What data does the program act upon?" Instead, you analyze the problem as a system of objects interacting. The first question you ask is, "What are the objects?" or "What are the active entities in this program?"

Not only does object-oriented design begin from a different premise from procedural decomposition, it proceeds in a different manner. Procedural decomposition is a *top-down* approach, starting with an abstract view of the program and ending with a detailed view. However, object-oriented design is not a top-down technique. You do not first identify large classes and then break them down into smaller ones. Nor is it necessarily a bottom-up process, where you start with small classes and build up from them (though class libraries can be used for this kind of approach). Object-oriented design involves working at both high and low levels of abstraction at all stages.

Object-oriented design requires you to do the following:

- Identify the classes
- Assign attributes and behavior
- Find relationships between the classes
- Arrange the classes into hierarchies

While you should begin by performing these steps in the order shown, remember that object-oriented design is an *iterative* process. If you perform each step in the process just once, without regard for the later steps, it's unlikely that you'll create a useful set of classes. Each step in the process may alter the assumptions you used in a previous step, requiring you to go back and repeat that step with new information. This does not mean that you shouldn't give any thought to your initial design. A good initial design is always desirable and will speed up the development process. However, you should expect revisions to occur. You successively refine your class descriptions throughout the design process.

Identifying the Classes

The first step is to find the classes that the program needs. This is more difficult than identifying the primary function of a program. You cannot simply perform a procedural decomposition of the problem, take the resulting structure types or data structures, and make them into classes. Your classes must be the central, active entities in your program.

One technique for identifying classes is to write a description of the program's purpose, list all the nouns that appear in the description, and choose your classes from that list. This is a simplistic approach whose success depends on how well the original description is written, but it can help give you ideas if you are new to object-oriented design.

It's easiest to identify classes for a program that models physical objects. For example, if your program handles airline seating reservations, you probably need an Airplane class and a Passenger class. If your program is an operating system, a Device class for representing disk drives and printers is a likely candidate class.

However, many programs don't model physical entities. For these situations, you must identify the conceptual entities that the program manipulates. Sometimes these are readily identifiable: A Rectangle class and a Circle class are obvious candidates for a graphic drawing program. In other cases, these are not as easy to visualize. For example, a compiler might need a SyntaxTree class, and an operating system might need a Process class.

Less obvious candidates for classes are events (things that happen to an object) and interactions (things that happen between objects). For example, a Transaction class could represent things such as loans, deposits, or funds transfers in a bank program. A Command class could represent actions performed by the user in a program.

You may see possible hierarchies for your classes. If you've identified BinaryFile and TextFile as candidate classes, you might derive them from a base class called File. However, it is not always obvious when a hierarchy is appropriate. For instance, a bank program could use a single Transaction class, or it could use separate Loan, Deposit, and Transfer classes derived from Transaction. As with the classes themselves, any hierarchies identified at this stage are simply candidates to be refined or discarded later in the design process.

All of the above candidate classes are meant to model elements in the problem you're trying to solve. Your program may also need another category of candidate classes: those that can be used to implement the other classes you've found. For instance, you may have identified a class that can be implemented using the SortedList class that you previously wrote. In that case, SortedList becomes a candidate class, even if your program description didn't explicitly mention sorted lists. In general, it is too early to think about how each class should be implemented, but it is appropriate to find ways to build classes using existing class libraries.

Assigning Attributes and Behavior

Once you've identified a class, the next task is to determine what responsibilities it has. A class's responsibilities fall into two categories:

- The information that an object of that class must maintain. ("What does an object of this class know?")

- The operations that an object can perform or that can be performed on it. ("What can this object do?")

Every class has "attributes," which are the properties or characteristics that describe it. For example, a Rectangle class could have height and width attributes, a GraphCursor class could have a shape (arrow, cross hairs, etc.), and a File class could have a name, access mode, and current position. Every instance of a class has a "state" that it must remember. An object's state consists of the current values of all its attributes. For example, a File object could have the name FOO.TXT, the access mode "read-only," and the position "12 bytes from the beginning of the file." Some attributes may never change value, while others may change frequently. An attribute's value can be stored as a data member, or it can be computed each time it is needed.

It is important not to confuse attributes and classes; you should not define a class to describe an attribute. A Rectangle class is useful, but Height and Width classes probably are not. Deciding whether to have a Shape class is not so easy. When a shape is used only to describe a cursor's state, it is an attribute. If a shape has attributes that can have different values, and a set of operations that can be performed on it, then it should be a class in itself. Moreover, even if a program needs a Shape class, other classes may still have shape as an attribute. The Shape objects that a program manipulates are unrelated to the shape of a GraphCursor object.

Every class also has "behavior," which is how an object interacts with other objects and how its state changes during those interactions. There is a wide variety of possible behaviors for classes. For example, a `Time` object can display its current state without changing it. A user can push or pop elements off a `Stack` object, which does change its internal state. One `Polygon` object can intersect with another, producing a third.

When deciding what a class should know and what it can do, you must examine it in the context of the program. What role does the class play? The program as a whole has information that makes up its state, and behavior that it performs, and all of those responsibilities must be assigned to one class or another. If there is information that no class is keeping, or operations that no class is performing, a new class may be needed. It is also important that the program's work be distributed fairly evenly among classes. If one class contains most of the program, you should probably split it up. Conversely, if a class does nothing, you should probably discard it.

The act of assigning attributes and behaviors gives you a much clearer idea of what constitutes a useful class. If a class's responsibilities are hard to identify, it probably does not represent a well-defined entity in the program. Many of the candidate classes found in the first step may be discarded after this step. If certain attributes and behavior are repeated in a number of classes, they may describe a useful abstraction not previously recognized. It may be worthwhile to create a new class containing just those characteristics, for other classes to use.

One common mistake among programmers new to object-oriented programming is to design classes that are nothing more than encapsulated processes. Instead of representing types of objects, these classes represent the functions found by a procedural decomposition. These false classes can be identified during this stage of the design by their lack of attributes. Such a class doesn't store any state information; it just has behavior. If, when describing a class's responsibilities, you say something like, "This class takes an integer, squares it, and returns the result," you have a function. Another characteristic of such classes is an interface consisting of just one member function.

Once you've identified the attributes and behavior of a class, you have some candidate member functions for the class's interface. The behavior you've identified usually implies member functions. Some attributes require member functions to query or set their state. Other attributes are only apparent in the class's behavior.

The specific member functions and their parameters and return types won't be finalized until the end of the design process. Furthermore, implementation issues play only a small role in the design process at this point. These include questions such as deciding whether attributes should be stored or computed, what type of representation should be used, and how to implement the member functions.

Finding Relationships Between Classes

The immediate extension of the previous step, deciding the features of each class, is deciding how the classes use each other's features. While some of the classes you identify can exist in isolation, many of them cannot. Classes build upon and cooperate with other classes.

Often one class depends upon another class because it cannot be used unless the other class exists. This is necessary when one class calls the member functions of the other class. For example, a `Time` class may have functions that provide conversions between it and a `String` object. Such functions must call the constructor and access functions of the `String` class.

Another way one class can depend on another is when it has the other class embedded within it, meaning that it contains objects of the other class as members. For example, a `Circle` object might have a `Point` object representing its center, as well as an integer representing its radius.

This type of relationship is called a "containing relationship." Classes that contain other classes are "aggregate" or "composite" classes. The process of containing member objects of other classes, known as "composition," is described in Chapter 4, "Introduction to Classes." Composition is sometimes confused with inheritance; the distinction between these two is discussed in the next section, "Arranging Classes into Hierarchies."

Most relationships between classes arise because one class's interface depends on another. For example, the class `Circle` may have a `getCenter` function that returns a `Point` object, so users must know about `Point` to use `Circle`'s interface. However, it is also possible for a class's implementation to depend on another class. For example, you might design `AddressBook` with a private member object of the `SortedList` class. Users of `AddressBook` don't need to know anything about `SortedList`. They need only know about the interface of `AddressBook`. This provides another layer of encapsulation, because it is possible to change the implementation of `AddressBook` without changing the interface.

When identifying relationships, you must consider how a class performs its assigned behavior. Does it need to know information that is maintained by other classes? Does it use the behavior of other classes? Conversely, do other classes need to use this class's information or behavior?

As you define the relationships between classes more fully, you'll probably modify some of the decisions you made in previous steps. Information or behavior that was previously assigned to one class may be more appropriate in another. Don't give objects too much information about their context. For example, suppose you have a Book class and a Library class for storing Book objects. There's no need for a Book object to know which Library holds it; the Library objects already store that information. By adjusting the borders between classes, you refine your original ideas of each class's purpose.

You might be tempted to use friend classes when you have one class that needs special knowledge about another class. However, the friend mechanism in C++ should be used very sparingly, because it breaks the encapsulation of a class. Modifying one class may require rewriting all its friend classes.

After identifying the relationships that one class has with others, you reach a closer approximation of the class's interface. You know which attributes require member functions to set them and which attributes require only query functions. You have a clearer idea of how best to divide the class's behavior into separate functions.

Arranging Classes into Hierarchies

Creating class hierarchies is an extension of the first step, identifying classes, but it requires information gained during the second and third steps. By assigning attributes and behavior to classes, you have a clearer idea of their similarities and differences; by identifying the relationships between classes, you see which classes need to incorporate the functionality of others.

One indication that a hierarchy might be appropriate is the use of a **switch** statement on an object's type. For example, you might design an Account class with a data member whose value determines whether the account is a checking or savings account. With such a design, the class's member functions might perform different actions depending on the type of the account:

```
class Account
{
public:
    int withdraw( int amount );
    // ...
private:
    int accountType;
    // ...
};
```

```
int Account::withdraw( int amount )
{
    switch ( accountType )
    {
    case CHECKING:
        // perform checking-specific processing
        break;
    case SAVINGS:
        // perform savings-specific processing
        break;
    // ...
    };
}
```

A **switch** statement such as this usually means that a class hierarchy with polymorphism is appropriate. As described in Chapter 7, "Inheritance and Polymorphism," polymorphism lets you call member functions for an object without specifying its exact type, by using virtual functions.

In the example above, the Account class can be made into an abstract base class with two derived classes, Savings and Checking. The withdraw function can be declared virtual, and the two derived classes can each implement their own version of it. Then you can call withdraw for an object without examining the object's precise type.

On the other hand, a hierarchy isn't needed just because you can identify different categories of a class. For example, is it necessary to have Sedan and Van as derived classes of Car? If you perform the same processing for every type of car, then a hierarchy is unnecessary. In this case, a data member is appropriate for storing the type of car.

Composition vs. Inheritance

Both composition and inheritance enable a class to reuse the code of another class, but they imply different relationships. Many programmers automatically use inheritance whenever they want to borrow the functionality of an existing class, without considering whether inheritance accurately describes the relationship between their new class and the existing one. Composition should be used when one class *has* another class, while inheritance should be used when one class *is* a kind of another class. For example, a circle is not a kind of point; it *has* a point. Conversely, a numeric data field does not contain a generic data field; it *is* a data field.

Sometimes it is difficult to determine whether inheritance or composition is appropriate. For example, is a stack a kind of list with a special set of operations, or does a stack contain a list? Is a window a kind of text buffer that can display itself, or does a window contain a text buffer? In such cases, you have to examine how the class fits in with the other classes in your design.

One indication that inheritance is the appropriate relationship is when you want to use polymorphism. With inheritance, you can refer to a derived object with a pointer to its base class and call virtual functions for it. With composition, however, you cannot refer to a composite object with a pointer to one of its member classes, and you cannot call virtual functions.

If you want to borrow another class's functionality more than once, composition is probably more appropriate. For example, if you're writing a `FileStamp` class and you want each object to store a file's creation date, last modification date, and last read date, composition is clearly preferable to inheritance. Rather than use a complicated multiple inheritance design, it's much simpler to include three `Date` objects as members.

Designing Classes for Inheritance

Building class hierarchies usually involves creating new classes as well as modifying or discarding ones previously identified. Most of the classes identified during the first step are probably ones that you intend to instantiate. However, when the common features of several classes are isolated, they often don't describe a class that is useful to instantiate. As a result, the new classes you create when forming a hierarchy may be abstract classes, which are not meant to have instances.

Adding abstract classes increases the ability to reuse a class. For example, you might create one abstract class that five classes inherit from directly. However, if two of those deriving classes share features that the others don't, those features can't be placed in the base class. As a result, they would have to be implemented in each class they appeared in. To prevent this, you can create an intermediate abstract class that is itself derived from the base but adds new features. The two classes can inherit their shared characteristics from this class. This also gives you greater flexibility when extending the hierarchy later on.

However, abstract classes should not be created indiscriminately. As an extreme example, it's possible to create a series of abstract classes, each of which inherits from another and adds only one new function. While in theory this promotes reusability, in practice it creates a very clumsy hierarchy.

It is desirable to place common features as high in a hierarchy as possible to maximize their reuse. On the other hand, you should not burden a base class with features that few derived classes use. Attributes and behavior may be shifted up and down the hierarchy as you decide which features should be placed in a base class.

Inheritance not only affects the design of class hierarchies, it can also affect the design of classes that stand alone. Any class you write might later be used as a base class by another programmer. This requires a refinement to the distinction between a class's interface and implementation. A class has two types of clients: classes or functions that use the class, and derived classes that inherit from the class. When designing a class, you must decide whether you want to define different interfaces for these two types of clients. The **protected** keyword enables you to make members visible to the derived classes but not to the users. You can thus give derived classes more information about your class than you give users.

A protected interface can reveal information about a class's implementation, which violates the principle of encapsulation. Modifying the protected portion of a class means that all derived classes must be modified too. Accordingly, the **protected** keyword should be used with care.

Multiple Inheritance

Multiple inheritance can be useful for maximizing reuse while avoiding base classes with unnecessary functionality. For example, remember the example of the abstract base class `SortableObject`, which has the interface that a class needs in order to be stored in a `SortedList`. Now consider a similar abstract base class called `PrintableObject`, which has an interface that all printable classes can use. You might have some classes that are printable, some that are sortable, and some that are both. Multiple inheritance lets you inherit the properties you need from the abstract base classes.

This scenario is difficult to model using only single inheritance. To avoid duplicating functions in different classes, you'd have to define a base class `PrintableSortableObject` and derive all your other classes from it. Certain classes would have to suppress the functions of the printable interface, while others would have to suppress the functions of the sortable interface. Such a class hierarchy is top-heavy, having too much functionality in its base class.

Virtual base classes are often used in hierarchies built around multiple inheritance. One drawback of virtual base classes, besides the processing overhead they entail, is that the need for them only becomes apparent when you design an entire hierarchy at once. Consider the example of the `SalesManager` class in Chapter 7, "Inheritance and Polymorphism." The need to make `Employee` a virtual base class doesn't arise until `SalesManager` is defined. If you didn't define `SalesManager` before the other classes were used in many programs, you must modify the existing hierarchy, causing extensive recompilation. If modifying the hierarchy isn't practical, you must use some other solution instead of virtual base classes.

Just as with single inheritance, multiple inheritance is often used inappropriately. Many situations where multiple inheritance is used are better modeled with composition or with a combination of composition and single inheritance. You should always examine one of these options when considering multiple inheritance.

Appendixes

C Language Guide

This appendix provides a quick summary of C language fundamentals. It does not attempt to teach you the C language or document all the details of C. Use it as a refresher or ready reference if you've previously learned the C language but haven't programmed in it recently.

For a complete description of the C programming language, see the *C Language Reference* online.

General Syntax

A C statement consists of keywords, expressions, and function calls. A statement always ends with a semicolon. A statement block is a collection of statements enclosed by braces ({ }). A statement block can appear anywhere a simple C statement appears. No semicolon occurs after the closing brace.

C is a free-format programming language. You can insert "whitespace" characters (spaces, tabs, carriage returns, and form feeds) almost anywhere, to indent statement blocks and otherwise make your code more readable.

Comments begin with the slash-asterisk sequence (/*) and end with the asterisk-slash sequence (*/). Comments are legal anywhere a space is legal, but they cannot be nested.

User-Defined Names

You can define your own names ("identifiers") for variables, functions, and user-defined types. Identifiers are case sensitive. For instance, the identifier `myVariable` is not the same as the identifier `Myvariable`.

You cannot use a C keyword (see the list below) as an identifier.

An identifier can contain only the following characters:

- abcdefghijklmnopqrstuvwxyz
- ABCDEFGHIJKLMNOPQRSTUVWXYZ
- 0123456789
- _ (underscore)

The first character of an identifier must be a letter or the underscore character. The Microsoft C compiler allows 247 characters in an identifier name.

Keywords

A keyword has a special meaning in the C language. You must spell keywords as shown in the following tables, and you cannot use them as user-defined names (see above).

The C language uses the following keywords:

auto	double	int	struct
break	else	long	switch
case	enum	register	typedef
char	extern	return	union
const	float	short	unsigned
continue	for	signed	void
default	goto	sizeof	volatile
do	if	static	while

The following keywords and special identifiers are recognized by the Microsoft C compiler:

_ _asm	dllimport[2]	_ _int8	naked[2]
_ _based[1]	_ _except	_ _int16	_ _stdcall
_ _cdecl	_ _fastcall	_ _int32	thread[2]
_ _declspec	_ _finally	_ _int64	_ _try
dllexport[2]	_ _inline	_ _leave	

[1] The _ _based keyword has limited uses for 32-bit target compilations.

[2] These are special identifiers when used with _ _declspec; their use in other contexts is not restricted.

A few other words, such as **main**, have a special meaning but are not keywords in the strict sense. Consult the *C Language Reference* online to get details on all such words.

Functions

Every C program must have at least one function, named **main**, which marks the beginning and end of the program's execution. Every executable statement in a C program must occur within a function.

Variables can be declared inside or outside functions. Variables declared inside a function are "local" and can be accessed only in that function. Variables declared outside all functions are "global" and can be accessed from any function in your program.

You call a C function by stating its name. If the function requires "arguments" (data), you list the arguments in the parentheses that follow the function name. Arguments that you pass to a function become local variables in the function.

A function can return a value (using the **return** keyword) or return nothing. If the function contains no **return** statement, it ends automatically when execution reaches the closing brace of the function definition.

A function "prototype" (declaration) tells the C compiler the function's name, the type of value it returns, and the number and type of arguments it requires. Function prototypes normally appear near the beginning of the program. They allow the compiler to check the accuracy of every reference to the function.

Flow Control

The C language provides several kinds of flow-control statements. The **for**, **while**, and **do** statements create loops. The **if** and **switch** statements perform a branch. The **break**, **continue**, **return**, and **goto** statements perform an unconditional "jump" to another location in your program.

The following sections describe the C flow-control statements in alphabetical order.

The break Statement

The **break** statement terminates the smallest enclosing **do**, **for**, **switch**, or **while** statement in which it appears. It passes control to the statement following the terminated statement.

This statement is often used to exit from a loop or **switch** statement (see below). The following example illustrates **break**:

```
while( c != 'Q' )
{
    /* Some C statements here */
    if( number_of_characters > 80 )
        break;  /* Break out of while loop */
    /* More C statements here */
}
/* Execution continues here after break statement */
```

The continue Statement

The **continue** statement is the opposite of the **break** statement. It passes control to the next iteration of the smallest enclosing **do**, **for**, or **while** statement in which it appears.

This statement is often used to return to the start of a loop from within a deeply nested loop.

The following example illustrates **continue**:

```
while( c != 'Q'
{
    /* Some C statements here*/
    if( c == 0x20 )
        continue;   /* Skip rest of loop */
    /* More C statements here */
}
```

In the example, the **continue** statement skips to the next iteration of the loop whenever c equals 0x20, the ASCII value for a space character.

The do Statement

The **do** statement repeats a statement until a specified expression becomes false. The test expression in the loop is evaluated after the body of the loop executes. Thus, the body of a **do** loop always executes at least once.

Use a **break**, goto, or **return** statement when you need to exit a **do** loop early. Use the **continue** statement to terminate an iteration without exiting the loop. The **continue** statement passes control to the next iteration of the loop.

The following example illustrates **do**:

```
sample = 1;
do
    printf( "%d\t%d\n", sample, sample * sample );
while( ++x <= 7 );
```

The **printf** statement in the example always executes at least once, no matter what value x has when the loop begins.

The for Statement

The **for** statement lets you repeat a statement a specified number of times. It consists of three expressions:

- An initializing expression, which is evaluated when the loop begins
- A test expression, which is evaluated before each iteration of the loop
- A modifying expression, which is evaluated at the end of each iteration of the loop

These expressions are enclosed in parentheses and followed by the loop body —the statement the loop is to execute. Each expression in the parentheses can be any legal C statement.

The **for** statement works as follows:

1. The initializing expression is evaluated.

2. As long as the test expression evaluates to a nonzero value, the loop body is executed. When the test expression becomes 0, control passes to the statement following the loop body.

3. At the end of each iteration of the loop, the modifying expression is evaluated.

You can use a **break**, **goto**, or **return** statement to exit a **for** loop early. Use the **continue** statement to terminate an iteration without exiting the loop. The **continue** statement passes control to the next iteration of the loop.

The following example illustrates **for**:

```
for( counter = 0; counter < 100; counter++ )
{
    x[counter] = 0; /* Set every array element to zero */
}
```

The goto Statement

The **goto** statement performs a jump to the statement following the specified label. A **goto** statement can jump anywhere within the current function.

A common use of **goto** is to exit immediately from a deeply nested loop. For instance:

```
for( ... )
{
    for( ... )
    {
        /* Do something here */
        if(c == CTRL_C)
            goto myplace;
    }
    /* Do something else here */
}

/* The goto label is named myplace myplace:  */
/* The goto statement transfers control here */
```

The if Statement

The **if** statement performs a branch based on the outcome of a conditional test. If the test expression is true, the body of the **if** statement executes. If it is false, the statement body is skipped.

The **else** keyword is used with **if** to form an either-or construct that executes one statement when the test expression is true and another when it's false. C does not offer an "else-if" keyword. You can combine **if** and **else** statements to achieve the same effect. C pairs each **else** with the most recent **if** that lacks an **else**.

Below is a simple **if** statement:

```
if( score < 70 )
    grade = 'F';
else
    grade = 'P';
```

If the value of the variable score is less than 70, the variable grade is set to the constant F. Otherwise, score is set to P.

The return Statement

The **return** statement ends the execution of the function in which it appears. It can also return a value to the calling function. For example:

```
return; /*End function and return no value */
return myvariable; /* End function and return value of myvariable */
```

The switch Statement

The **switch** statement allows you to branch to various sections of code based on the value of a single variable. This variable must evaluate to a **char**, **int**, or **long** constant.

Each section of code in the **switch** statement is marked with a case label—the keyword **case** followed by a constant or constant expression. The value of the **switch** test expression is compared to the constant in each case label. If a match is found, control transfers to the statement after the matching label and continues until you reach a **break** statement or the end of the **switch** statement.

For example:

```
switch( answer )
{
    case 'y': /* First case */
    printf( "lowercase y\n" );
    break;

    case 'n': /* Another case */
    printf( "lowercase n\n" );
    break;

    default:  /* Default case */
    printf( "not a lowercase y or n\n" );
    break;
}
```

The example tests the value of the variable answer. If answer evaluates to the constant 'y', control transfers to the first case in the **switch** statement. If it equals 'n', control transfers to the second case.

A case labelled with the **default** keyword executes when none of the other case constants matches the value of the **switch** test expression. In the example, the **default** case executes when answer equals any value other than 'y' or 'n'.

If you omit the **break** statement at the end of a case, execution falls through to the next case.

If you omit the **default** case and no matching case is found, nothing in the **switch** statement executes.

No two **case** constants in the same **switch** statement can have the same value.

The while Statement

The **while** statement repeats a statement until its test expression becomes false. A **while** loop evaluates its test expression before executing its loop body. If the test expression is false when the loop begins, the loop body never executes. (Contrast this behavior with the **do** loop, which always executes its loop body at least once.)

For example:

```
while( !sample )   /* Repeat until sample equals 1 */
{
    printf( "%d\t%d\n", x, x*x );
    x += 6;
    if( x > 20 )
        sample = 1;
}
```

You can exit a **while** loop early with a **break** or **goto** statement. The **continue** statement skips to the next iteration of the loop.

Data Types

Data types are explained in more detail in the *C Language Reference* online. A brief description is given here.

Basic Data Types

The basic data types in C are character (**char**), integer (**int**), and floating point (**float** and **double**). All other data types are derived from these basic types. For example, a string is an array of **char** values.

Microsoft C recognizes the types shown in the table below.

Table A.1 Basic Data Types

Type Name	Bytes	Other Names	Range of Values
int	*	**signed,** **signed int**	System dependent
unsigned int	*	**unsigned**	System dependent
_ _int8	1	**char,** **signed char**	−128 to 127
_ _int16	2	**short,** **short int,** **signed short int**	−32,768 to 32,767
_ _int32	4	**signed,** **signed int**	−2,147,483,648 to 2,147,483,647
_ _int64	8	none	−9,223,372,036,854,775,808 to 9,223,372,036,854,775,807
char	1	**signed char**	−128 to 127
unsigned char	1	none	0 to 255
short	2	**short int,** **signed short int**	−32,768 to 32,767

Table A.1   Basic Data Types (*continued*)

Type Name	Bytes	Other Names	Range of Values
unsigned short	2	unsigned short int	0 to 65,535
long	4	long int, signed long int	−2,147,483,648 to 2,147,483,647
unsigned long	4	unsigned long int	0 to 4,294,967,295
enum	*	none	Same as int
float	4	none	3.4E +/- 38 (7 digits)
double	8	none	1.7E +/- 308 (15 digits)
long double	10	none	1.2E +/- 4932 (19 digits)

Character Type

The character type (**char**) occupies one byte of storage and can express a whole number in the range of −128 to 127. Unsigned characters have a range of 0 to 255. You can represent any ASCII character as an **unsigned char** value.

Typical declarations of character types are shown below:

```
char answer; /* Declare a character variable answer */

char alpha = 'a'; /* Declare character variable alpha and initialize it */
```

A character constant represents a single ASCII character. Typical character constants are shown below:

```
char alpha = 'a'; /* Declare and initialize */

char c2 = 0x61; /* Declare and initialize with hexadecimal value for 'a' */
```

Escape Sequences

Escape sequences represent special characters, such as the carriage return. An escape sequence consists of a backslash character plus a letter or punctuation mark. Escape sequences are listed below.

Table A.2   C Escape Sequences

Sequence	Name
\a	Alert (bell)
\b	Backspace
\f	Formfeed
\n	Newline
\r	Carriage return
\t	Horizontal tab
\v	Vertical tab

Table A.2   C Escape Sequences (*continued*)

Sequence	Name
Sequence	Name
\?	Literal question mark
\'	Single question mark
\"	Double quotation mark
\\	Backslash
\ddd	ASCII character in octal notation
\xdd	ASCII character in hex notation
\0	Null character

Integer Type

The int and unsigned int types have the size of the system word. This is two bytes (the same as short and unsigned short) in MS-DOS and 16-bit versions of Windows, and 4 bytes in 32-bit operating systems. However, portable code should not depend on the size of int.

Integer variables are declared with the keywords **int**, **short**, **unsigned**, or **long**. Typical declarations of integer types are shown below:

```
int z; /* Declare an int variable z */

int ten = 10; /* Declare int variable and assign it the value 10 */

unsigned int a; /* Declare unsigned int variable */

unsigned long BigInt = 2000000001UL; /* Declare and initialize */
```

Integer constants are used to represent decimal, octal, and hexadecimal numbers. There are three types of integer constants:

1. Decimal constants can only contain the digits 0–9. The first digit must not be 0.

2. Octal constants can only contain the digits 0–7. The first digit must be 0.

3. Hexadecimal constants can only contain the digits 0–9, plus the letters a–f or A–F. The constant must begin with either 0x or 0X.

You can specify that an integer constant is long by adding the suffix **1** or **L**. The suffix can be used with decimal, hexadecimal, or octal notation.

To specify that an integer constant is short, add the suffix **u** or **U**. This suffix can also be used with decimal, hexadecimal, or octal notation.

Typical integer constants are shown below:

```
42       /* Decimal constant */

0x34        /* Hexadecimal constant */

052      /* Octal constant */

0x3cL    /* Long hexadecimal constant */
```

Floating-Point Types

You can declare floating-point variables using the keywords **float** or **double**. The **float** type occupies four bytes of storage and can express a floating-point value in the range 3.4E−38 to 3.4E+38. This type has seven-digit precision.

The **double** type occupies eight bytes of storage and can express a floating-point value in the range 1.7E−308 to 1.7E+308. This type has fifteen-digit precision.

The **long double** type occupies ten bytes of storage and can express a floating-point value in the range 1.2E−4932 to 1.2E+4932. This type has nineteen-digit precision.

Typical declarations of floating-point types are shown below:

```
float SmallPi = 3.14;    /* Declare floating-point variable */

double AccuratePi = 3.141592653596    /* Declare double-precision */
```

Floating-point constants can represent decimal numbers in either single or double precision. A floating-point constant must either contain a decimal point or end with the suffix **e** or **E**. Typical floating-point constants are shown below:

```
2.78    /* Floating-point constant */

3E  /* Floating-point constant */
```

Aggregate Data Types

Aggregate data types are built from one or more of the basic data types. These include the following:

- Arrays (including strings)
- Structures
- Unions

Arrays and Strings

An "array" is a collection of data elements of a single type. An array can contain any data type. You can access an element of an array by using the array name and a numeric subscript.

A "string" is an array of characters that terminates with the null character (\0). Arrays that contain strings must allow space for the final null character.

Typical arrays and strings are shown below:

```
int id_number[10]; /* One-dimensional; 10 elements; integer */

char name[30]; /* String */

float matrix[5][3]; /* Two-dimensional array, 5 rows, 3 columns */

char baby[30] = "Peter Roddy"; /* String initialization */
```

Structures

A "structure" is a collection of data items of different types. Once you have defined a structure type, you can declare a structure variable using that type.

The following example illustrates a simple structure:

```
struct date

{
    int month;
    int day;
    int year;
}

struct date today;
```

The example defines a structure type named date and declares a structure variable today to be of type date.

Use the structure-member operator (.) to access the "elements" (members) of a structure. The name

```
today.month
```

refers to the month member of the today structure in the example.

Unions

A "union" is a set of data items of different types sharing the same storage space in memory. For instance:

```
union UNKNOWN
{
    char    ch;
    int     i;
    long    l;
    float   f;
    double  d;
};
```

The size of this union is eight bytes, which is the size of the union's largest member (the member of type **double**).

Advanced Data Types

Advanced data topics are explained in the *C Language Reference* online. A brief description of each topic is given here.

Visibility

Variables declared outside all functions are global and can be accessed anywhere in the current source file. Variables declared inside a function are local and can be accessed only in that function. Use the **extern** keyword to make a variable declared in another source file visible in the current source file.

Lifetime

Global variables, and local variables declared with the **static** keyword, exist for the lifetime of the program. Other local variables are "automatic"; they come into being when the function starts and evaporate when it ends.

Type Conversions

A type conversion occurs automatically when an expression mixes two different data types. C converts the lower-ranking type to the higher-ranking type before it performs the specified operation.

You can also "cast" (manually convert) a value to any type by placing the desired type name in parentheses in front of the value. The example below casts the value of sample to type **float** and assigns the value to x:

```
int sample;
float x;
x = (float)sample;
```

User-Defined Types

The **typedef** keyword allows you to create user-defined types, which are synonyms for existing data types. User-defined types can make your program more readable. For example, a type called string may be easier to understand than a type called **char ***.

A simple **typedef** declaration is shown below. The name of an existing type (**long int**) is followed by the synonym income.

```
typedef long int income;
```

Once you have created a new type name, you can use it wherever the original type name could be used:

```
income net_income, gross_income;
```

In the example above, the variables `net_income` and `gross_income` are of type `income`, which is the same as **long int**.

Enumerated Types

An enumerated type (declared with **enum**) has values limited to a specified set. If the **enum** declaration does not specify any values, C assigns sequential integers to the enumeration identifiers beginning at zero.

The example below assigns the values of 0, 1, and 2 to the enumeration identifiers `zero`, `one`, and `two`, respectively.

It also creates an enumerated type `small_numbers` that can be used to declare other variables.

```
/* Enumerated data type */
enum small_numbers {zero, one, two};

/* Variable my_numbers is of type small_numbers */
enum small_numbers  my_numbers;
```

The following example explicitly assigns values to the enumeration identifiers:

```
/* Enumerated data type */
enum even_numbers { two = 2, four = 4, six = 6 };
```

Operators

An "operand" is a constant or variable manipulated by an operator in an expression. An "operator" specifies how the operands in an expression are to be evaluated. Operators also produce a result that can be nested within a larger expression.

C provides a rich set of operators covering everything from basic arithmetic operations to logical and bitwise operations. You can also combine the assignment operator (=) with any arithmetic or bitwise operator to form a combined assignment operator.

C operators have two properties, precedence and associativity. You can change the normal order of evaluation by enclosing expressions in parentheses.

The table below lists the C operators and their precedence and associativity values. The lines separate precedence levels. The highest precedence level is at the top of the table.

Table A.3   C Operators

Symbol	Name or Meaning	Associativity
Highest Precedence		
++	Post-increment	Left to right
--	Post-decrement	
( )	Function call	
[ ]	Array element	
->	Pointer to structure member	
.	Structure or union member	
++	Pre-increment	Right to left
--	Pre-decrement	
!	Logical NOT	
~	Bitwise NOT	
-	Unary minus	
+	Unary plus	
&	Address	
*	Indirection	
sizeof	Size in bytes	
(type)	Type cast [for example, (float)i]	
*	Multiply	Left to right
/	Divide	
%	Remainder	
+	Add	Left to right
-	Subtract	
<<	Left shift	Left to right
>>	Right shift	
<	Less than	Left to right
<=	Less than or equal to	
>	Greater than	
>=	Greater than or equal to	
==	Equal	Left to right
!=	Not equal	
&	Bitwise AND	Left to right
^	Bitwise exclusive OR	Left to right
		Bitwise OR	Left to right
&&	Logical AND	Left to right

Table A.3   C Operators (*continued*)

Symbol	Name or Meaning	Associativity
||	Logical OR	Left to right
? :	Conditional	Right to left
=	Assignment	Right to left
*=, /=, %=, +=, -=, <<=, >>=, &=, ^=, |=	Compound assignment	
,	Comma	Left to right

Lowest Precedence

Preprocessor Directives

A "preprocessor directive" is a command to the C compiler, which processes all such commands before it compiles your source program. A preprocessor directive begins with the # symbol, followed by the directive and any arguments the directive needs. Since a preprocessor directive is not a C language statement, it doesn't end in a semicolon.

The two most commonly used directives are **#define** and **#include**. Use the **#define** directive to give a meaningful name to some constant in your program. The following directive tells the compiler to replace PI with 3.14159 everywhere in the source program:

```
#define PI   3.14159
```

The **#include** directive below tells the compiler to insert the contents of a specified file at the current location in your source program.

```
#include <stdio.h>   /* Standard header file */
```

Such files are called "include files" or "header files." Standard header files, such as STDIO.H, end with the .H extension and contain function prototypes and other definitions needed for C library routines.

See the *Run-Time Library Reference* online for information on the header files needed by individual library functions.

Pointers

A "pointer" is a variable that contains the memory address of an item rather than its value. A pointer can point to any type of data item or to a function. The following code illustrates pointer declarations:

```
int *intptr; /* Pointer to an integer */
char *name; /* Pointer to char */
```

The following operators are used with pointers:

- The indirection operator (*) has two uses. In a declaration, it means that the declared item is a pointer. In an expression, it denotes the data being pointed to.

- The address-of operator (**&**) yields the memory address at which an item is stored.

You can perform four arithmetic operations on pointers:

1. Adding a pointer and an integer
2. Subtracting an integer from a pointer
3. Subtracting two pointers
4. Comparing two pointers

Pointer arithmetic operations are automatically scaled by the size of the object pointed to. For instance, adding 1 to a pointer to a **float** item causes the address stored in the pointer to be incremented four bytes, the size of one **float** item.

Programming Pitfalls

In C, as in every language, it's rare for any program to work perfectly the first time. An important part of knowing a language is recognizing what *not* to do and why certain problems occur.

This appendix describes common C programming pitfalls and how to avoid them. It is organized under broad topics, such as "Pointer Problems," with a category for miscellaneous problems at the end. The description of each error gives a code example, explains why the error occurs, and offers a solution.

Note The examples in this appendix are described in the context of the C language. Because of the differences between C and C++, the C++ compiler may display error messages that are different from the ones described here when compiling these examples.

Operator Problems

The most common operator problems involve operators unique to C. Others involve questions of precedence, which can cause problems in any language.

Confusing Assignment and Equality Operators

A common error is to confuse the assignment operator (=) with the equality operator (==). The mistake often occurs in decision-making statements:

```
int val = 555;
if( val = 20 )    /* Error! */
    printf( "val equals 20\n" );
```

The above code prints `val equals 20` even though it's clear `val` doesn't equal 20 when the **if** statement begins. Instead of testing whether x equals 20, the expression `val = 20` *assigns* the value 20 to `val`.

Remember, the single equal sign (=) performs an assignment in C. This particular assignment results in a nonzero value, so the **if** test is evaluated as true, causing the **printf** statement to execute.

To correct the problem, use the double equal sign (==) to test equality:

```
if( x == 20 )
    printf( "x equals 20\n" );
```

Once you're in the habit of using the equality operator, you might make the opposite mistake of using two equal signs where you should use only one:

```
#include <stdio.h>

void main()
{
    int val;
    for( val == 0; val < 5; val++ )   /* Error! */
        printf( "val = %d\n", val );
}
```

Here the error appears in the initializing expression of the **for** statement. It's the reverse of what happened in the first example. Instead of assigning the value 0 to val, the expression val == 0 evaluates whether or not val equals 0. The expression doesn't change the value of val at all. Since val is an uninitialized variable, the **for** loop is unpredictable.

Confusing Operator Precedence

Peculiar things can happen if you ignore operator precedence:

```
#include <conio.h>
#include <stdio.h>

void main()
{
    int ch;
    while( ch = getch() != '\r' )
        printf( "%d\n", ch );
}
```

Instead of assigning the result of the **getch** library-function call to ch, the above code assigns the value 0 to ch when you press the ENTER key and the value 1 when you press any other key. (The values 1 and 0 represent true and false.)

The error occurs because the inequality operator (!=) has higher precedence than the assignment operator (=). The expression

```
ch = getch() != '\r'
```

is the same as

```
ch = (getch() != '\r')
```

Both expressions compare the result of the **getch** call to the character constant **\r**. The result of that comparison is then assigned to ch.

For the program to work correctly, these operations must happen in the reverse order. The result of the function call must be assigned to the variable *before* the variable is compared to the constant. We can solve the problem by adding parentheses:

```
#include <conio.h>
#include <stdio.h>

void main()
{
    int ch;
    while( (ch = getch()) != '\r')
        printf( "%d\n", ch );
}
```

Parentheses have the highest precedence of any operator, so the expression

```
(ch = getch()) != '\r'
```

works correctly. It assigns the result of the **getch** call to ch before comparing ch to the constant.

The list of precedence-related errors is almost endless. To view a complete table of operator precedences, see Appendix A, "C Language Guide," and the *C Language Reference* online.

When in doubt, use extra parentheses to make the order of operations absolutely clear. Extra parentheses don't degrade performance, and they can improve readability as well as minimize precedence problems.

Confusing Structure-Member Operators

Two different operators are used to access the members of a structure. Use the structure-member operator (**.**) to access a structure member directly, and the pointer-member operator (**–>**) to access a structure member indirectly through a pointer.

For instance, you may create a pointer to a structure of the employee type,

```
struct employee *p_ptr;
```

and initialize the pointer to point to the jones structure:

```
p_ptr = &jones;
```

If you use the structure-member operator to access a structure member through the pointer,

```
p_ptr.months = 78; /* Error! */
```

the C compiler issues this error message:

```
C2231: left operand points to 'struct', use '->'
```

Use the pointer-member operator to access a structure member through a pointer:

```
p_ptr->months = 78;
```

Array Problems

The most common errors associated with arrays involve indexing errors. The problems described in this section all concern indexing errors of one form or another.

Array Indexing Errors

If you're used to a language that has different subscripting rules, it's easy to forget that the first subscript of a C array is 0 and the last subscript is 1 less than the number used to declare the array. Here's an example:

```
#include <stdio.h>

int i_array[4] = { 3, 55, 600, 12 };
void main()
{
    int count;
    for( count = 1; count < 5; count++ )   /* Error! */
        printf( "i_array[%d] = %d\n", i_array[count] );
}
```

The **for** loop in the above program starts at i_array[1] and ends at i_array[4]. It should begin with the first element, i_array[0] and end at the last, i_array[3]. The following corrects the error:

```
for( count = 0; count < 4; count++ )
    printf( "i_array[%d] = %d\n", i_array[count] );
```

Omitting an Array Subscript in Multidimensional Arrays

Programmers who know Basic, Pascal, or Fortran may be tempted to place more than one array subscript in the same pair of brackets. In C, each subscript of a multidimensional array is enclosed in its own pair of brackets:

```
#include <stdio.h>

int i_array[2][2] = { { 12, 2 }, { 6, 55 } };
void main()
{
    printf( "%d\n", i_array[ 0, 1 ] ); /* Error! */
}
```

In the preceding example, the expression

```
i_array[ 0, 1 ]
```

does not access element 0,1 of i_array. Here is the correct way to refer to that array element:

```
i_array[0][1]
```

Interestingly, the deviant array reference doesn't cause a syntax error. It's legal to separate multiple expressions with a comma operator, and the final value of such a series is the value of the rightmost expression in the group. Thus, the expression

```
i_array[ 0, 1 ]
```

is equivalent to this one:

```
i_array[ 1 ];
```

Both expressions give an address, not the value of an array element.

Overrunning Array Boundaries

Since C doesn't check array subscripts for validity, you must keep track of array boundaries on your own. For instance, if you initialize a five-character array,

```
char sample[] = "ABCD";
```

and refer to a nonexistent array element,

```
sample[9] = 'X';
```

The C compiler doesn't signal an error, although the second statement overwrites memory outside the array. It stores a character in element 9 of an array that contains only 5 elements.

The same problem can occur when accessing an array through a pointer:

```
char sample[] = "ABCD";
char *ptr = sample;
*--ptr = 'X';   /* Error! */
```

The code overwrites the byte in memory below the array. To avoid such problems, confine all array operations within the range used to declare the array.

String Problems

Strings are handled a little differently in C than most languages—a fact that can cause problems. The following errors are common to programs that use strings.

Confusing Character Constants and Character Strings

Remember the difference between a character constant, which has one byte, and a character string, which is a series of characters ending with a null character:

```
char ch = 'Y';
if( ch == "Y" )  /* Error! */
    printf( "The ayes have it..." );
```

The example above mistakenly compares the **char** variable ch to a two- character string ("Y") instead of a single character constant ('Y'). Since the comparison is false, the **printf** statement never executes—no matter what ch equals.

The **if** statement needs to use single quotes. This code correctly tests whether ch equals the character 'Y':

```
char ch = 'Y';
if( ch == 'Y' )
    printf( "The ayes have it..." );
```

Forgetting the Null Character That Terminates Strings

Remember that strings end with a null character in C. If you declare this five-character array,

```
char sample[5];
```

the compiler allocates five bytes of memory for the array. If you try to store the string "Hello" in the array like this,

```
strcpy( sample, "Hello" );
```

you'll overrun the array's bounds. The string "Hello" contains six characters (five letters and a null character), so it's one byte too big to fit in the sample array. The **strcpy** overwrites one byte of memory outside the array's storage.

It's easy to make this error when allocating memory for a string, too:

```
char str[] = "Hello";
char *ptr;
ptr = malloc( strlen( str ) );   /* Error! */
if( ptr == NULL )
    exit( 1 );
else
    strcpy( ptr, str );
```

This time the error occurs in the call to the **malloc** function, which allocates memory to a pointer prior to a string copy. The **strlen** function returns the length of a string not including the null character that ends the string. Since the amount of memory allocated is one byte too small, the **strcpy** operation overwrites memory, just as in the previous example.

To avoid the problem, add 1 to the value returned by **strlen**:

```
ptr = malloc( strlen( str ) + 1 );
```

Forgetting to Allocate Memory for a String

If you declare a string as a pointer, don't forget to allocate memory for it. This example tries to create a **char** pointer named `ptr` and initialize it with a string:

```
#include <string.h>

void main()
{
    char *ptr;
    strcpy( ptr, "Ashby" );  /* Error! */
}
```

The pointer declaration `char *ptr;` creates a pointer variable but nothing else. It allocates enough memory for the pointer to store an address but doesn't allocate any memory to store the object to which `ptr` will point. The **strcpy** operation in the next line overwrites memory by copying the string into an area not used by the program.

One way to allocate memory is by declaring a **char** array large enough to hold the string:

```
#include <string.h>

void main()
{
    char c_array[10];
    strcpy( c_array, "Randleman" );
}
```

You can also call the **malloc** library function to allocate memory at run time:

```
#define BUFFER_SIZE 30
#include <stdio.h>
#include <string.h>
#include <malloc.h>

void main()
{
    char *ptr;
    if( ptr = (char *) malloc( BUFFER_SIZE ) )
    {
        strcpy( ptr, "Duvall" );
        printf( ptr );
        free( ptr );
    }
}
```

Pointer Problems

Every experienced C programmer has a collection of favorite pointer-induced bugs. Pointer errors can wreak havoc because pointers can change the contents of any addressable memory location. If a pointer writes to an unexpected address, the results can be disastrous.

Using the Wrong Address Operator to Initialize a Pointer

If you're still learning about pointers, it's easy to forget which address operator to use when initializing a pointer variable. For example, you might want to create a pointer to a simple **int** variable:

```
int val = 25;
int *ptr;
ptr = val; /* Error! */
```

The code above doesn't initialize `ptr` correctly. Instead of assigning to `ptr` the address of `val`, the statement

```
ptr = val;
```

tries to assign `ptr` the contents of `val`, causing an warning:

```
warning C4047: '=' : 'int *' differs in levels of indirection from 'int'
```

Because `val` is an **int** variable, its contents can't form a meaningful address for `ptr`. You must use the address-of operator to initialize `ptr`:

```
ptr = &val;
```

Here's another pointer initialization error:

```
int val = 25;
int *ptr;
*ptr = &val; /* Error! */
```

The last line doesn't initialize `ptr` to point to the variable `val`. The expression to the left of the equal sign, `*ptr`, stands for the object `ptr` points to. Instead of assigning `ptr` the address of `val`, the line tries to assign the address of `val` to the integer that `ptr` points to. This assignment triggers a message similar to the message above:

```
warning C4047: '=' : 'int' differs in levels of indirection from 'int *'
```

Here is the correct way to initialize this pointer:

```
ptr = &val;
```

Using Dangling Pointers

A "dangling pointer" is one that points to a memory area no longer in use by your program. Dangling pointers, like uninitialized pointers, can be very dangerous to use.

For instance, say you allocate a block of memory with the **malloc** library function:

```
#define BUFSIZE 1000
char *ptr;
if( ptr = (char *) malloc( BUFSIZE ) )
    /* do something */ ;
```

After the memory block has been allocated with **malloc**, the pointer ptr points to a valid data object. Once you're done using allocated memory, you normally return it to the heap:

```
free( ptr );
```

After you free the memory it points to, ptr is a dangling pointer. It still points to a valid machine address, but that address is no longer in use by the program. You shouldn't use the pointer at this stage, just as you shouldn't use it before it has been initialized.

Dangling pointers can also be created by a function that returns a pointer to a local variable:

```
int *boo_boo( void )
{
    int object;
    .
    .
    .
    return &object; /* Error! */
}
```

The boo_boo function returns the address of the local variable object, forgetting the storage for object is no longer part of the program after the function ends.

Here's a variant of the previous example involving a string pointer:

```
char *boo_boo( void )
{
    char *c_ptr;
    c_ptr = "Hello";
    .
    .
    .
    return c_ptr; /* Error! */
}
```

Since the string constant "Hello" is local to the function, it evaporates when the function ends, leaving the pointer c_ptr dangling.

Library-Function Problems

Once you've learned enough about C to write practical programs, you can begin to explore the C run-time library. This section outlines a few common problems related to using library functions. Again, you can use online help to get information about specific library functions.

Failing to Check Return Values from Library Functions

Almost all library functions return some value e—either the result of processing or an error code showing success or failure. You should always check library-function return values, even if you're confident of the result.

This rule is critical when calling a library function such as **malloc**, which allocates memory at run time:

```
char *ptr;
ptr = (char *) malloc( BUFSIZE );   /* Error! */
```

If the call to **malloc** fails, the pointer `ptr` is assigned a null (0) value. Using `ptr` under these circumstances can overwrite unexpected memory addresses or cause a run-time error. The following code checks the return value from **malloc**:

```
#define NULL 0
#define BUFSIZE 32768
        .
        .
        .
char *ptr;
if( (ptr = (char *) malloc( BUFSIZE ) ) != NULL )
{
    printf( "Copacetic.\n" );
    /* Do something useful... */
}
else
    printf( "Not enough memory!\n" );
```

Duplicating Library-Function Names

There are so many functions in the C run-time library that it's sometimes difficult to avoid duplicating function names. For instance, if you write a function that reads data from a buffer, the name `read` may strike you as short and descriptive.

The only problem is that **read** is the name of a C run-time library function. A program that defines its own `read` function may work correctly at first, but if you later include the header file that declares the **read** library function,

```
#include <io.h>
```

then redefinition errors occur. You can't use the same name for two different functions. The solution here is to rename the user-defined function.

Visual C++'s online help lets you check for such name conflicts on the spot. Put the cursor on the function name you wish to use, then press F1. If the name is already used for a library function, online help displays information about the function. If the name isn't in online help, it's not used in the C run-time library and is a safe choice.

Unless you're writing your own library functions, it's a good rule to avoid declaring names that begin with an underscore (_), since many of the system-defined names in C start with that character. (Non-ANSI library functions begin with a single underscore. Predefined identifiers such as _ _**TIME**_ _ start with two underscores, and routines internal to the C run-time library can begin with either one or two underscores.)

Forgetting to Include Header Files for Library Functions

Because they contain needed function prototypes, it's important to include the correct header files when using C run-time library functions:

```
#include <stdio.h>

void main()
{
    double val = sqrt( (double) 10 );
    printf( "square root of 10 = %le\n", val );
}
```

The program above calls the library function **sqrt**, which calculates a square root. Most of the program is correct. When passing the value 10 to **sqrt**, it casts the argument as a **double**, the type **sqrt** expects. The return value from **sqrt** is assigned to a **double** variable, too.

Unfortunately, the program still gives the wrong output. The square root of 10 is not 3.2 (3.200000e+001 in exponential notation):

```
square root of 10 = 3.200000e+001
```

Because the program has no prototype for the **sqrt** function, **sqrt** has the **int** return type by default. The value returned by **sqrt** undergoes an unexpected type conversion—from type **double** to **int**—and significant digits are lost.

This problem is easily solved. Simply include the standard header file that contains the prototype for **sqrt**:

```
#include <stdio.h>
#include <math.h>
void main()
{
    double val = sqrt( (double) 10 );
    printf( "square root of 10 = %le\n", val );
}
```

Now the program works correctly:

```
square root of 10 = 3.162278e+000
```

If you're not sure which header file a library function needs, take advantage of the online help. (Put the cursor on the function name and press F1.) If the function needs a header file, the file name appears in an **#include** directive above the function prototype.

Omitting the Address-Of Operator When Calling scanf

Don't forget to put the address-of operator in front of arguments when using the **scanf** library function (the **scanf** function accesses keyboard input):

```
#include <stdio.h>

void main()
{
    int val;
    printf( "Type a number: " );
    scanf( "%d", val ); /* Error! */
    printf( "%d", val );
}
```

When the program calls **scanf**, it omits the address-of operator that should precede the second argument:

```
scanf( "%d", val );  /* Error! */
```

The **scanf** function expects to be passed a pointer to a variable (in this case, a pointer to val) so it can assign an input value to the variable. But because the address-of operator is missing, the program passes the value of val, not its address.

Instead of storing an input value in val as intended, **scanf** uses the uninitialized value of val as a pointer and assigns the input value to an unpredictable address. As a result, val remains uninitialized and the program overwrites memory elsewhere—two very undesirable events.

Here is the correct way to call **scanf** in this program:

```
scanf( "%d", &val );
```

Macro Problems

Function-like macros— macro definitions that take arguments— share many of the advantages of functions. They can cause unwanted side effects, however, if you fail to put parentheses around their arguments or carelessly supply an argument that uses an increment or decrement operator.

Omitting Parentheses from Macro Arguments

A macro definition that doesn't enclose its arguments in parentheses can create precedence problems:

```
#include <stdio.h>

#define FOURX(arg)  ( arg * 4 )
void main()
{
    int val;
    val = FOURX( 2 + 3 );
    printf( "val = %d\n", val );
}
```

The FOURX macro in the program multiplies its argument by 4. The macro works fine if you pass it a single value, as in

```
val = FOURX( 2 );
```

but returns the wrong result if you pass it this expression:

```
val = FOURX( 2 + 3 );
```

The C compiler expands the above line to this line:

```
val = 2 + 3 * 4;
```

Because the multiplication operator has higher precedence than the addition operator, this line assigns val the value 14 (or 2 + 12) rather than the correct value 20 (or 5 * 4).

You can avoid the problem by enclosing the macro argument in parentheses each time it appears in the macro definition:

```
#include <stdio.h>

#define FOURX(arg)  ( (arg) * 4 )
void main()
{
    int val;
    val = FOURX(2 + 3);
    printf( "val = %d\n", val );
}
```

Now the program expands this line

```
val = FOURX(2 + 3);
```

into this one:

```
val = (2 + 3) * 4;
```

The extra parentheses assure that the addition is performed before the multiplication, giving the desired result.

Using Increment and Decrement Operators in Macro Arguments

If a function-like macro evaluates an argument more than once, you should avoid passing it an expression that contains an increment or decrement operator:

```
#include <stdio.h>
#define ABS(value)  ( (value) >= 0 ? (value) : -(value) )

void main()
{
    int array[4] = {3, -20, -555, 6};
    int *ptr = array;
    int val, count;
    for( count = 0; count < 4; count++ )
    {
        val = ABS(*ptr++); /* Error! */
        printf( "abs of array[%d] = %d\n", count, val );
    }
}
```

The program uses a macro named ABS, which returns the absolute value of the argument you pass to it.

The goal in this program is to display the absolute value of every element in array. It uses a **for** loop to step through the array and a pointer named ptr to access each array element in turn. Instead of the output you would expect,

```
abs of array[0] = 3
abs of array[1] = 20
abs of array[2] = 555
abs of array[3] = 6
```

the program gives this output:

```
abs of array[0] = -20
abs of array[1] = -6
abs of array[2] = 8307
abs of array[3] = 24864
```

(The last two array values may differ if you run the program. They are the contents of memory not used by the program.)

The error occurs in this line,

```
val = ABS(*ptr++); /* Error! */
```

which the C compiler expands as shown here:

```
val = ( (*ptr++) >= 0 ? (*ptr++) : -(*ptr++) ); /* Error! */
```

Because it uses the conditional operator, the ABS macro always evaluates its argument at least twice. This isn't a problem when the argument is a constant or simple variable. In the example, however, the argument is the expression *ptr++.

Each time the macro evaluates this expression, the increment operator takes effect, causing ptr to point to the next element of array.

The first time the program invokes the macro, ptr points to the first array element, array[0]. Since this element contains a nonnegative value (3) the macro evaluates the argument twice. The first evaluation takes the value that ptr points to and then increments ptr. Now ptr points to the second element, array[1]. The second evaluation takes the value of array[1] and increments ptr again.

The first macro invocation not only returns an incorrect value (−20, the value of array[1]), it also leaves ptr pointing to the third array element, making the results of later invocations unpredictable. (The pointer eventually moves past the last element of array and points to unknown data.)

To avoid the problem, don't use the increment or decrement operators in arguments you pass to a macro. This revision removes the error by incrementing ptr in the **for** statement instead of the macro invocation:

```
#include <stdio.h>
#define ABS(value)  ( (value) >= 0 ? (value) : -(value) )

void main()
{
    int array[4] = {3, -20, -555, 6};
    int *ptr = array;
    int val, count;
    for( count = 0; count < 4; count++, ptr++ )
    {
        val = ABS(*ptr);
        printf( "abs of array[%d] = %d\n", count, val );
    }
}
```

This advice applies generally to C run-time library routines as well as macros you write. Remember, some run-time library routines are implemented as macros rather than C functions. If you're not sure whether a library routine is actually a macro, look it up in online help.

Miscellaneous Problems

This section describes C programming problems that don't fit into any convenient category.

Mismatching if and else Statements

In nested **if** statements, each **else** is associated with the closest preceding **if** statement that does not have an **else**. Although indentation can make nested constructs more readable, it has no syntactical effect:

```
if( val > 5 )
    if( count == 10 )
        val = sample;
else
    val = 0;
```

The indentation suggests that the **else** associates with the first **if**. In fact, the **else** is part of the second **if**, as shown more clearly here:

```
if( val > 5 )
    if( count == 10 )
        val = sample;
    else
        val = 0;
```

The **else** is part of the second **if** statement—the closest preceding **if** that doesn't have a matching **else**. To tie the **else** to the first **if**, you must use braces:

```
if( val > 5 )
{
    if( count == 10 )
        val = sample;
}
else
    val = 0;
```

Now the **else** belongs with the outermost **if**. Remember, indentation is meaningful only to humans. The compiler relies strictly on punctuation when it translates the source file.

Misplacing Semicolons

Misplaced semicolons can cause subtle bugs:

```
#include <stdio.h>

void main()
{
    int count;
    for( count = 0; count < 500; count++ ); /* Error! */
    {
        printf( "count = %d\n", count );
        printf( "And the beat goes on...\n" );
    }
}
```

You might expect the program to print the value of count 500 times, but this is all it prints:

```
count = 500 And the beat goes on...
```

The culprit is the extra semicolon immediately after the parentheses of the **for** statement. Its effect is more evident if we reformat the statement:

```
#include <stdio.h>

void main()
{
    int count;
    for( count = 0; count < 500; count++ )
        ; /* Null statement */
    {
        printf( "count = %d\n", count );
        printf( "And the beat goes on...\n" );
    }
}
```

Instead of printing the value of count 500 times, the program executes the null statement (;) 500 times. Null statements are perfectly legal in C, so the compiler has no way to tell this is a mistake.

Since the null statement is interpreted as the loop body, the **printf** statements inside curly braces are interpreted as a statement block and executed once. Statement blocks usually appear as part of a loop, function definition, or decision-making statement, but it's legal to enclose any series of statements in braces.

The program works as intended if you remove the extra semicolon:

```
#include <stdio.h>

void main()
{
    int count;
    for( count = 0; count < 500; count++ )
    {
        printf( "count = %d\n", count );
        printf( "And the beat goes on...\n" );
    }
}
```

Here's another one. If you know Pascal, you might be tempted to put a semicolon after the parentheses of a function definition:

```
void func( void );

void func( void ); /* Error! No semicolon here. */
{
    printf( "C is not Pascal\n" );
}
```

The function header causes a syntax error. While a function declaration requires a semicolon after its parentheses, a function definition does not. This code corrects the error:

```
void func( void );

void func( void )
{
    printf( "C is not Pascal\n" );
}
```

Omitting Double Backslashes in Pathname Specifications

Because C uses the backslash (\) as an escape character, it's easy to create garbled path specifications:

```
fp = fopen( "c:\temp\bodkin.txt", "w" );
```

At first glance, the path specification in the string

```
"c:\temp\bodkin.txt"
```

looks good because that's how you would type it on the command line. In a quoted string, however, the backslash is interpreted as an escape character. In this string the sequences \t and \b are interpreted as the tab and backspace character, respectively, garbling the path and file name. Even if the indicated file exists, this call to **fopen** is sure to fail.

In a quoted string the escape sequence for a backslash character is a double backslash (\\). This statement solves the problem:

```
fp = fopen( "c:\\temp\\bodkin.txt", "w" );
```

Omitting break Statements from a switch Statement

Don't forget to include **break** statements when using the **switch** statement:

```
switch( ch )
{
    case 'e':
        printf( "Bye bye\n" );
        break;
    case 'l':
        printf( "Loading the file\n" );
        load_file( fp );
        break;
    case 's':
        printf( "Saving the file\n" );
        write_file( fp );  /* Error! Missing break. */
```

```
   case 'd':
      printf( "Deleting the file\n" );
      kill_file( fp );
      break;
   default:
      break;
}
```

In this code a **break** statement is missing from the statements following the third case label (the statements that print `Saving the file`). After those statements execute, execution falls through to the next case label, deleting the newly saved file.

To avoid this problem, place a **break** at the end of every case item:

```
case 's':
   printf( "Saving the file.\n" );
   write_file( fp );
   break;
```

It's legal, of course, to write a program in which execution deliberately falls through from one case label to the next. In such cases you may want to add a comment to prevent confusion.

Mixing Signed and Unsigned Values

If you explicitly compare two values of different types, the compiler normally catches the error. Some type mismatches aren't easy to spot, however, even for humans:

```
#include <stdio.h>

#define CHARVAL '\xff'

void main()
{
    unsigned char uc;
    uc = CHARVAL;
    if( uc == CHARVAL )
       printf( "Eureka!" );
    else
       printf( "Oops..." );
}
```

The program prints `Oops...` which probably wasn't expected. The comparison between `CHARVAL` and `uc` is false even though both are clearly **char** values.

The answer lies in the way the compiler converts **signed** and **unsigned char** values into **int** values for internal use. The **#define** directive,

```
#define CHARVAL '\xff'
```

defines `CHARVAL` as the constant 0xff. Since no sign is specified, the compiler treats the constant as a **signed char** value by default. When it converts the **char** to an **int** for internal use, as it does all character values, the compiler extends the value's sign. The result is an **int** with the value 0xffff.

The variable uc undergoes the same internal conversion, with an important difference. Since uc is explicitly declared as **unsigned**, its value is converted to an **int** value of 0x00ff.

When the two **int** values are compared, the result is false (0xffff does not equal 0x00ff). One solution is to explicitly cast CHARVAL to the desired type:

```
#define CHARVAL (unsigned char)'\xff'
```

Now the compiler compares two **unsigned char** values, giving the desired result. Another solution is to make CHARVAL an **int** instead of a **char** constant:

```
#define CHARVAL 0xff
```

Both solutions give the desired result, although the second is slightly less efficient. It creates word-size, rather than byte-size, machine-code instructions.

Index